Handbook of the public libraries of Manchester and Salford

William E. A. 1846-1913 Axon

HUMFREDUS CHETHAM ARMIGER, *FUNDATOR*

Natus 10 Julii 1580. Obiit 12 Octobris 1653.

HANDBOOK

OF THE

PUBLIC LIBRARIES

OF

MANCHESTER AND SALFORD.

By WILLIAM E. A. AXON.

MANCHESTER:
ABEL HEYWOOD AND SON,
56 AND 58, OLDHAM STREET.

SIMPKIN, MARSHALL, AND CO., LONDON.

1877.

TO

JOHN HOWARD NODAL,

A STEADFAST FRIEND

OF THE STUDIES THAT PUBLIC LIBRARIES CAN AID,

THIS VOLUME,

WHICH WOULD NOT HAVE BEEN WRITTEN

BUT FOR HIS ENCOURAGEMENT,

IS DEDICATED.

PREFACE.

———◆———

THE present volume is an attempt to show the nature of the collections to be found in the public libraries of Manchester and Salford. The object has been the practical one of stating in the concisest form, as an aid to investigators, the salient points in each library. The description of books of special interest to biliophiles and bibliomaniacs has been kept subsidiary to the general purpose thus indicated. Whilst it would have been easier to have taken the rarer volumes and to have noticed them in detail, it seemed more useful to indicate the lines of study and research which each collection could best aid. The greater portion of the work has appeared at intervals in the *Manchester City News*, whence it is now reprinted with additional articles and an appendix. An index containing references to all the authors and subjects named in the text will, it is hoped, aid the reader.

The writer has to express his obligations to the officials of the various libraries for facilities of examination. He has also to thank Mr. C. W. Sutton and Mr. J. H. Nodal for valuable suggestions.

BANK COTTAGE,
  BARTON-ON-IRWELL.

CONTENTS.

APPENDIX.

———◆———

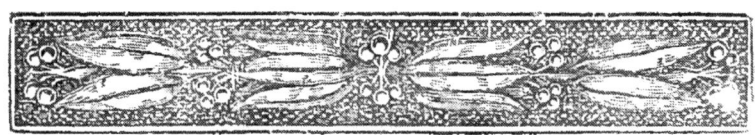

PUBLIC LIBRARIES IN MANCHESTER.

I. THE CHETHAM.

The public library founded by Humphrey Chetham is one of the very few relics left of Old Manchester. The story of the building has often been told, and of its successive transformations until it became, by the munificent spirit of the Manchester merchant, a house for orphans, and an abiding place for the literary riches of past ages. The Chetham library was the first in Europe to open its doors freely to all comers without distinction of rank or creed. Access to its most precious possessions is offered to all, without more restriction than is implied in the applicant writing his name in the register kept for the purpose. The hours during which it is open are longer now than in former years, though it is still unfortunately closed in the evening. It is open from 10 a.m. to 6 p.m. in summer, and from 10 a.m. to 4 p.m. in winter.

The number of volumes in the collection is about 38,000. The collection of printed books shows by the disproportionate number of folios that it was

commenced in another age than this. Some of these
books are dead beyond all hope of resurrection. The
ponderous tomes of the schoolmen will meet with
few readers now. It would, however, be wrong to
suppose, as is sometimes done, that the Chetham
library is a mere receptacle of ancient theology.
Chacun à son gout, and there are still some who
would sooner read Bishop Pilkington than Mr.
Spurgeon; but even those who do not care for
" schoolmen or divines," and are proof against the
seductions of the Benedictine Patres Bibliotheca
will find something to their taste. The
student of history will be delighted with the fine
series of national chronicles of Italy, France, Den-
mark, Bohemia, Austria, and Germany, the lover of
finely illustrated books with the Antichita di Erco-
lano, the Museum Florentinum, Salvini's Hindoos,
Hamilton's Etruscan Antiquities, and with the
splendid works on natural history by Le Vaillant,
Agassiz, Gould, and Roscoe. Amongst the modern
works throwing light upon the history of the past of
our own country may be named a complete set of the
chronicles and calendars of State Papers published
by the Master of the Rolls. These important
works are numerous enough to fill a separate book-
case. A fine set of Tom Hearne's works, extending
to three score volumes, offers much fine pasture for
the lovers of that miscellaneous antiquary. For our
American cousins we may name John Frampton's
English translation of the "Joyfull Newes out of the
new - founde Worlde," written by Monardus in
Spanish, and the original edition of Richard
Hakluyt's voyages.

There are not so many early printed books as perhaps might have been expected, but examples are here from the presses of Jenson, Aldus, and Wynkyn de Worde, and William Caxton. Amongst these books the first printed edition of Homer should be noticed. Printed at Florence in 1488 it "displays" (to quote Gibbon) "all the luxury of the typographical art."

One great use of public libraries is to serve as storehouses for those great literary productions which, from their size and cost, are beyond the reach of all book-lovers and students who do not happen to be millionaires. The Bollandist "Acta Sanctorum" is a collection of lives of the Saints, arranged in months. It was commenced in 1643, has now got down to the month of October, and fills three score volumes. Amongst other mighty works, we may name that recording the proceedings of the French Academy; Zedler's Lexicon, in sixty-four vols. folio; the Gentleman's Magazine from 1731; the British Critic, 100 vols.; the Monthly Review, 182 vols.; and the Journal de Trevoux, the last-named curious periodical extending to 333 volumes. There are many works which one would like to mention, but as the object of these papers is rather to indicate materials for lines of study than to enumerate curiosities, they may be passed over.

The tracts include a volume of plays by Thomas Heywood and others, and a very extensive series on the Romanist Controversy under James II. These letters are enumerated in

A Catalogue of the Collection of Tracts for and against Popery, published in or about the reign of James II., in

the Manchester Library founded by Humphrey Chetham
Edited by Thomas Jones, B.A., librarian. Printed for the
Chetham Society, 1859 65 ; quarto, two volumes

There is a series of tracts on the Essentialist Dispute,
and another on an earlier phase of the Catholic
Controversy. As Manchester was an early strong-
hold of Swedenborgianism, the magnificent edition
of his Autographa issued in facsimile should be
mentioned.

Students of Shakspere should examine the wonderful edition of his works published by Mr. Halliwell, and if they study him by the light of the age
in which he lived, an almost indispensable aid is
the edition of the Registers of the Stationers' Company, just issued by Mr. Arber. The Chetham is
the only public library in the district possessing this
important and expensive work.

BYROM LIBRARY.

On the death of Miss Atherton, his last lineal
descendant, the books of Dr. Byrom, the famous
Jacobite and stenographer, came to the library. A
full list of them is given in

A Catalogue of the Library of the late John Byrom,
Esq , M.A , F R S , preserved at Kersall Cell, Lancashire.
Printed for private circulation only. 1848.

This was compiled by Thomas Rodd, when the collection was still at Kersall Cell. Some of the books
are in poor condition, but they are interesting
as reflecting the mental features of their collector. There are some interesting local books,
and some now rare works on shorthand.
The strength of the Byrom collection lies, however,
in its many works of English and foreign mystics.

Whether it be a fine edition of the Imitatio Christi or the prophecies of Kotterus and Poniatowski that is wanted there is a fair chance of its being found on these shelves. A copy of Tyndall's New Testament is worth naming, and we may add that both the Byrom and the general collection contain some notable exemplars of Biblical works. There are a few MSS., amongst them the works of Paracelsus, and Gui de Chauliac, and a beautiful fifteenth century copy of Aulus Gellius.

HARLAND'S SHORTHAND COLLECTION.

The late Mr. John Harland, F.S.A., contemplated writing a history of shorthand, and made extensive collections with that view. His shorthand library, ranges from Shelton (1637 to 1641) downwards, and includes the systems of ninety distinct authors. Whilst Mr. Harland's shorthand library has come here, his MS. collections for a history of that art have found a resting place in the Free Library.

THE HALLIWELL BROADSIDE COLLECTION.

In 1851 the library received, by the liberality of Mr. Halliwell, a very remarkable collection of fugitive pieces of various ages. They include every variety of this class from a royal proclamation to a street ballad. There is a separate list of them.

Catalogue of proclamations, broadsides, ballads and poems, presented to the Chetham Library, Manchester, by J. O. Halliwell. London: 1851. Printed for private circulation.

This is simply an enumeration of the pieces as they have been pasted into their respective volumes without any regard to classification. The earliest is an indulgence promised to the benefactors of St.

George's Church, Southwark, and is supposed to have come from the press of Wynkyn de Worde. The strength lies not so much in ballad literature as in the *pièces volantes*, relating to trade and commerce. There is, however, an interesting series of (comparatively) modern street songs. The collection contains altogether 3,100 articles.

MANUSCRIPTS.

The Chetham Library has a small collection of Oriental Manuscripts. Amongst them are Firdusi's Shah-Nameh, and an abridgement of the Mahabharata. It is to be regretted that these MSS. have not been thoroughly examined and described by some orientalist. The Hafiz MS. has been used in:

Persian Lyrics, poems from the Divan-i-Hafiz; with paraphrases; a Catalogue of the Gazels as arranged in a MS. of the works of Hafiz in the Chetham Library, and other illustrations. By John Haddon Hindley London 1800. Quarto.

The European MSS. are more numerous and more important. The gem of the collection is a copy of the Flores Historiarum of Matthew Paris, partly in the handwriting of that chronicler himself. Besides the artistic interest of its illuminations it has thus a literary importance from its value as a text. Its money value is probably not over-estimated when put at a thousand pounds. There is a Wycliffite New Testament dating from 1430; an inedited Venetian relation of England; a curious poetical common-place book, which has been printed by Mr. Grosart; a unique copy of Torrent of Portyngle. Some of Richard of Hampole's work; a fifteenth century MS. of Alain Chartier; and many others which must be passed in silence. Amongst the more recent accessions is an extensive work by the late Mr. S. Leigh Sotheby—a Bibliographical Account of the printed works of the English Poets, in six volumes folio. This was prepared for publication by its learned author, and consists of transcripts of title pages, collations, rates of the auction prices, and so forth, but usually at least, without literary comment. The MSS. were described in a small pamphlet published by Mr. Halliwell over thirty years ago, but a new edition would now be welcome :—

An Account of the European Manuscripts in the Chetham Library, Manchester. By James Orchard Halliwell, F.R.S., Manchester, 1842.

LOCAL COLLECTIONS.

The antiquary investigating the history of this district will find much to help him in the special collections here. Under the names of Barritt, Hampson, Piccope, Kuerden, Hollingworth, Palmer, and others, will be found much matter that still remains inedited. There are several fine scrap-books filled with miscellanea relating to Lancashire, one of them containing a complete set of Mr. Harland's antiquarian contributions to periodicals. Amongst earlier material may be named the Addlington MS. and the Rate-book for Lancashire, compiled by William Crabtree. In this connection may be mentioned the portraits of Bradford, Nowell, and Chetham in the reading-room, Nowell's Commonplace-book, the Bible of Bradford the Martyr, and Dee's Book of Mysteries. A great store-house of local information is the set of the *Manchester Mercury* from 1752 to 1825.

The general catalogue of the Chetham collection is entitled .—

Bibliotheca Chethamensis ; sive Bibliothecæ Publicæ Mancuniensis ab Humfredo Chetham, armigero, fundatæ, catalogus Edidit Joannes Radcliffe, A M , Mancunii, 1791-1826. 2 vols. containing 6,723 entries Tom. III. Edidit Gulielmus Parr Greswell, Manc 1826 (ends with 8029). Tom. IV. Edidit Thomas Jones, B A , Oxon. Manc. 1862 (ends with 12058). Tomus V. Quatuor Catalogis Voluminum Index, sive notitia brevior unico tomo comprehensa. Edidit Thomas Jones, B.A., Manc 1863 Supplementary Index including the Addenda 1869.

The catalogue is a very useful one, the absence of an index of topics being its chief defect.

II.

THE PORTICO.

The Portico Newsroom and Library was founded in 1806. It is a social as well as a literary institution, and may perhaps be regarded as an early type of that luxury of civilization, the modern clubhouse. On passing through its gloomy portals, in Mosley-street, the visitor finds himself in a handsome reading-room. This room, devoted to newspapers, is lighted from the domed ceiling. A gallery, supported by iron pillars, runs round the room, and contains the library—undoubtedly the most valuable portion of the institution. There is also a room for periodicals.

The Portico is open from eight o'clock in the morning until nine in the evening, and the library portion from nine until six. The reading-room was formerly open also on the Sunday evening, but this practice has been abandoned. The institution is owned by four hundred shareholders, styled proprietors, each of whom has bought or inherited a share, and is liable for a yearly subscription of £2. 10s. The library and reading-room are open to the ladies of the respective families of the proprietors, and strangers are allowed to consult books in the library by a written order from a shareholder. This last regulation, we believe, has always been liberally construed, so that no one engaged in special researches which the stores of the Portico can aid is likely to be turned away. As a further evidence of literary sympathy we may add that one rule provides that the librarian of the Chetham Library shall be a honorary member of the Portico, and of its governing body.

The Portico Library is essentially modern in its character, and the scholarly flavour permeating it is of a different order to that of the Chetham Library. There is only one MS., but that is a very fine one, and was bought for the library by Mr. James Crossley at the Mainwaring sale. If it were in the market now, it would probably fetch not less than ten times the amount then paid for it. It is a large folio, consisting of 431 leaves of parchment, finely written, and with occasional illuminated letters. It contains five books of Valerius Maximus, the Latin text being accompanied by the French translation, that " Maistre Symon de Hesdin, maistre en theologie et frere de lospital de Saint Jehan de Jherusalem," made at the request of Charles V. of France. At the end of Book I. is the date of its completion, 1375, and the second book was accomplished two years later ; the remainder are undated. The volume merits a more detailed description than we can now give.

The strength of the Portico collection lies in its historical books, using that word in its wider sense. In this class we may name the magnificent "Description de l'Egypt," the result of the Napoleonic descent upon the land of Misraim. The two volumes of text and the dozen volumes of plates form a mine of wealth for those who care to dig therein. Gau's "Antiquités de la Nubie" is also here. Belonging to quite another branch of historical inquiry is Gayot de Pitaval's Causes Célèbres (Amsterdam, 1775), in twenty-six volumes. For the English student, there are the valuable series of chronicles and calendars published by the Master of the Rolls, supplemented by the works of many modern historians—by Rymer's Fœdera, Rushworth's Historical Collections, and other books of a similar character. The more exclusively antiquarian departments are fairly well filled—Du Cange, Baxter, and Spelman's Glossaries, Bartsch's Peintre Graveur, Dodd's Connoisseur's Repertorium, and Niceron's Hommes Illustres being all valuable, though in very different degrees. In topographical works the library is well supplied, the most notable books in this class being the first edition of Sir William Dugdale's Warwickshire, and a fine copy of Sir P. Leycester's Cheshire. In bibliography the library is not strong, both Quérard and Graesse being absent. Quérard's works, it is needless to say, are simply indispensable in studying the literary history of modern France. The bibliomaniacs may, however, delight themselves with the perusal of the catalogues of the wonderful libraries of Grenville, Heber, Earl Spencer, and the Duke of Sussex, or recreate in the pages of Auctioneer Robin's account of the "classic contents" of Strawberry Hill. A quarter of a century since this was stigmatised as the worst catalogue ever made, but "many things have happened since then." In this class we should name a very pleasant American magazine—"Philobiblion"—in which the dry bones of bibliography are made to live by the infusion of a literary spirit not always evident in such works. Baillet's Jugemens des Savans and Menage's Anti-Baillet should also be named.

In the publications of the learned societies and printing clubs, the Portico is at least moderately well supplied, having, amongst others, those of the Académie Royale des Sciences, the Irish Archæological, the Camden, Cavendish, Chetham, Royal Society (142 volumes), Royal Society of Edinburgh Shakspere, Astronomical, Ballad, Early English Text, Hakluyt, Royal Society of Literature, Palæontographical, Philological, Spenser, and Wodrow Societies, and of the British Association, American Philological Association, and others of less moment. The periodicals include sets of the European, Fraser, Dublin University, and New Monthly magazines. The scientific portion of the library, although including some valuable botanical works, is not so well filled as the historical.

Of the special collections, the most curious is that known as the Adlington Pamphlets, extending to 218 volumes. In the last century the pamphleteers exercised some of the influence now wielded by the journalists, and the various parties were eager for the services of those who could thus mould the public mind. Addison, Swift, and Steele were all political pamphleteers, whilst later we find Dr. Johnson, the leviathan of literature, thus disporting amongst the ministerial minnows. Mr. C. Leigh, of Adlington, by whom the collection was formed, seems to have been a man of varied tastes and wide culture, so that the tracts reflect a good deal, not only of the political, but of the literary and scientific aspects of the middle of the last century, the bulk of the tracts ranging from 1720 to 1760.

There are poems by Stephen Duck, the thresher, and plays by Voltaire, squibs against the Ministry and the Methodists, instructions for the destruction of vermin, and some tracts also written by human vermin, whom it is unlawful to destroy. Jest-books and farriery-books, profane plays, and pious sermons, jostle each other in charming confusion, and it may be that passing from a discourse on the reformation of manners we fall upon a batch of loose poems

> Each one warmer
> Than the former.

The very miscellaneous nature of the collection makes it all the more valuable as a reflex of the intellectual forces at work in the England of Hogarth and Byrom. Many of the works amongst the Adlington pamphlets are rare. Comparatively few of them are local, but one must be named in passing, and that is the first edition of Tim Bobbin, now become a bibliographical rarity of the first order. The British Museum has no copy of it, nor is it in any other public library in this city, although some few copies are known to exist in private collections. The original editions of Dr. Byrom's productions should not be passed over. It is to be regretted that there is no adequate catalogue of these tracts. Although they must number more than a thousand distinct articles they are dismissed in three lines of the printed catalogue. A smaller collection of miscellaneous pamphlets, ranging in date from 1808 to 1841, and extending to forty-five volumes, contains some interesting local matter. In this connection we may name also a set of Wheeler's *Manchester*

Chronicle from 1810 to 1843, and the *Chester Courant* from 1749 to 1753.

The indispensable guide—the eye of the library—is entitled " Catalogue of the Portico Library, Manchester. Printed by Cave and Sever, 1856. Octavo, pp. xvii, 570   Volume II. Manchester, 1875, pp. xiv, 554." On the appearance of the first volume it was assailed, in one quarter at least, with some justice and a good deal of hypercriticism.   The classification, although elaborate (its analysis occupies seventeen pages), is not satisfactory, if judged with logical severity, but, notwithstanding admitted " errors," " discrepancies," and " compromises," the catalogue has proved a fair working key to the books.   It would be an ungracious task to point out the errors which may be noticed in it, especially as on the whole they are not of a character to detract greatly from its usefulness.

III.

OWENS COLLEGE.

We hope that the future University of Manchester will have, amongst its other apparatus for culture, a magnificent library. What it possesses now, though by no means inconsiderable, is merely the nucleus of what such a collection of books should be. Before the library can fittingly aid the lecture-room very many sections in it, which at present make one think of Master Slender, will have to expand to the goodly proportions of fat Sir John.

The library, for its small size, has an unusual proportion of good valuable books. This is due in a great measure to the benefaction of the late Bishop Lee, who bequeathed his library to the college. It forms at once the most interesting and the most important part of the college library. A man's books to a certain extent mirror his character; they serve to indicate his intellectual sympathies if not his moral qualities. It is not without interest then to examine the silent friends of one who bulked so largely before the local world as the late Dr. Lee. The library will have its surprises. That it should evidence high scholarship will astonish none, but that it should have rich and rare books in the domain of the fine arts, that it should contain the Book of Mormon and the writings of Thomas Paine—that erewhile bogey of nervous Evangelicals—will be to some at least unexpected. The evidence of the books is greatly in the favour of their late owner. They are such as one would expect to find in the workshop of a scholar, anxious for accuracy

and thoroughness in his profession, and at the same
time blessed with no inconsiderable range of culture.
The almost entire absence of works of imagination,
including in that term the tender graces of Gold-
smith's Vicar and the "kind-hearted" plays of
Beaumont and Fletcher, might lead a rash theorist
to suppose that this defect gave a key to that hardness
which marred the character of the late prelate. But
we believe it would be incorrect to consider that
the collection now represents the library as it was
in the Bishop's prime, the books belonging to the
classes indicated having been sold previous to his
death. The Lee Library has a good catalogue prepared by Prof. A. W. Ward:

A Catalogue of the MSS and printed books bequeathed
to Owens College, Manchester, by the late Right Rev James
Prince Lee, D D, Lord Bishop of Manchester. Manchester, 1870. 8vo, pp 212.

The classification is very minute, and on the whole
satisfactory. It would perhaps have been as well to
have had a distinct class for biographical literature.
This would at least have shown how poor this important department is both in the Lee Bequest and
in the general library Some other details are open
to criticism.

In MSS. the collection is not very rich.
One of St Augustine of the twelfth century
may be named, and a Vulgate Bible of the
fourteenth century. There are also some
early Horæ. The most interesting, perhaps, to
us are the local MSS. The Bishop became possessed of the collections made by Mr. C. H.
Timperley, a man of prodigious industry, who at

one time projected a Palatine biography, to include notices of a thousand Lancashire worthies. It is almost pathetic to see the interest which Dr. Lee took in his diocese. There are many volumes of Scrapbooks which he has collected relating to it. There is a copy of Baines, swelled from four to fifteen volumes by the insertion of additional matter. In the same way the portion of Gastrell's Notitia, relating to the Bishop's diocese, has grown from one thin quarto volume into a gigantic work filling a dozen double folios. He apparently made a point of collecting such histories of the towns and villages in his diocese as came in his way. Amongst other local rarities may be cited Jackson's Mathematical Lectures, issued in 1719, and the first book printed in Manchester of which we have any certain information. Returning from this digression we may name a local MS.—a sermon preached in 1586, on the marriage of one of the Traffords.

The Theological department is, as one would naturally expect, very well filled. The editions of the Biblical codices are numerous. Not only is there the Codex Alexandrinus, but its rarer compeer the Codex Sinaiticus. Even the Codex Mayerianus of the forger Simonides has a place. Walton's Polyglot Bible should be named, and the works on the New Testament Apocrypha by Fabricius, Thilo, and others. There are also some interesting Biblical versions, some of them specimens of famous presses.

In Patristic literature the collection appears rich. The miscellaneous theology shows a liberal spirit, which could see the possibility of gaining help alike from St. Basil's homilies and the sermons of Dr.

Arnold.   There is a copy of Barrow's Remains—a
publication thus referred to in the bitter epigram on
Bishop Lee, circulated at his death :—

> Would you edit a book without learning or brains,
> You have only to look at his Barrow's Remains

Dr. Lee is said to have suppressed the book.   The
liturgical section is rich in forms of prayer.   Here
we may name also the Amsterdam edition of the
Mischna.   The section on the sacred writings of
other religions is very poorly filled, and so are the
classes on Mythology, which are placed in History,
but perhaps might have found a more appropriate
place here.   The works on general and comparative
philology show that the Bishop could sometimes
wander far afield.   In the classics of Greece and
Rome, it is rich and full, and will form a good basis
for an excellent library.   This and the study of the
Greek Testament were evidently his pet departments.
Oriental philology is very sparingly represented, although it includes Hebrew.   The mental and moral
sciences are represented by two score volumes, twelve
of them being the Bridgwater Treatises !   The
political and economical sciences fare a little better,
and include the valuable reprints of Lord Overstone.
The legal sciences are somewhat more adequately
represented.   The Corpus Juris Civilis, 1563, will
interest legal antiquaries, whilst the numerous works
on canon law, and on the laws of Britain, possess a
more immediately practical interest.   There are also
works on Chinese and Gentoo Law.

The class of history and geography (including
archæology) contains many fine works.   The Art de

Verifier les Dates may be named amongst the general treatises. The fine plates of Fergusson's Rock-cut Temples of India have a more than antiquarian interest. In English history we notice Domesday-book (1793), Matthew Paris (1640), the publications of the old Record Commission, a set (in 295 vols.) of Hansard's Debates, Tanner's Bibliotheca, and numerous "chronicles." Of the local histories we have already spoken. Amongst the books on ecclesiastical history and archæology are a Bullarium Romanum (1638), Huss and Jerome of Prague (1558), Le Plat's Council of Trent (1781), and Spelman's Concilia (1639 to '64). On prehistoric archæology there are but two works, one of them being the fine Atlas of the Ages of Bronze and Iron published by the Copenhagen antiquaries.

The scientific part of Bishop Lee's library cannot be considered as extensive. The classes of mathematics, natural philosophy, chemistry, natural history, medical science, mechanical arts, are all of them very inadequately filled. Under Montucla, Newton, Horrox, Leigh, Pettigrew, are articles worth looking at. Those who take an interest in tracing the history of the textile manufactures will be pleased to find here Mr. Yates' work on ancient weaving.

The class relating to the fine arts will prove an an agreeable surprise to many. It is not always that in the library of a hardworking classical scholar and theologian one finds so much space given up to the pictorial arts which add so greatly to the pleasures of life. After naming Canale's etchings, the Museum Florentinum, the engravings of Bartoli, the Monumenti Inediti, we can assure the lover of art that still there's more to follow.

We come now to the last class, that of general modern literature, which for the reason already indicated we do not think represents the Bishop's reading. Amongst the few bibliographical books we should name Kloss's catalogue of Melancthon's library. The only novelists here are Fielding and Mrs. Gaskell. Shakespere is represented by one play The publications of learned societies include those of the Antiquaires du Nord, Camden, Chetham, Manx, Ray, Sydenham, Dilettanti, Archælogical, Instituto di Corrispondenza Archeologica, Geographical, Royal, Literature, and several of the local societies.

Turning now from the Lee Bequest to the general library of the college we may premise that there is no printed catalogue, but a MS. one has been prepared, at a great cost of the time and labour of the librarian. Professor Ward's classification is adhered to, and his Lee catalogue forms an integral portion of it. We can only refer very briefly to the general library. In theology we notice the works by which Dr. Ginsburg is bringing to light the treasures of Hebrew learning; a number of works by Plymouth Brethren; Darrel's Survey, 1602; the works of John Huss, in their first edition; the sermons of Charlotte Rees, written before she was twelve years old; and the "Sermones" of the quaint free-spoken Geyler von Keisersberg, one of Luther's forerunners, who made the Strassburg Minster ring with his outcries against the sins of his day. Geyler was no vulgar ranter; his library was one of the best of its

day, and he left it to Strassburg for the advancement
of sound learning.   Here we name Schreiber's book
on the Strassburg Minster.   Noteworthy for very
different reasons is the work on polygamy, by
"Theophilus Alethæus," annotated by "Athanas.
Vincentius," both being the assumed names of
its author, Lyserus. Boeckh's Greek and Mommsen's
Latin Inscriptions are too important to be unnoticed.
The historical books are, for the most part, modern,
but we may mention the Parallelum Olivæ (1656),
the little work relating to Garnet as superior of the
English Jesuits, 1607, Naudé "Sur les Coups d'estat,"
Eric Olaus (1654), and Saxo Grammaticus (1644).
Those interested in the Gypsies will be glad to find
here Paspati's book, while those working at church
history may find something useful in Rémy-Cellier's
numerous quartos, or even in Orsini's "Histoire de
la Mère de Dieu."   Amongst the earlier scientific
books are Geber's works (1686), Tycho Brahe (1648),
and Harvey on the Circulation of Blood (1661). The
Chemical department seems to be very well filled, and
to be rich in the periodical literature of that science.
Finally we may notice that the library has some very
fine books on natural history.   Those who have seen
the pictorial wonders of Audubon, Wilson and
Bonaparte, and Le Vaillant's ornithological studies
alone can understand their beauty.   Some of these
natural history books have a local interest as in that
illustrating the Knowsley Menagerie and Aviary.

In 1874 the late Mr. C. J. Darbishire left the sum
of £1,000 for the extension of the library, the sum
spent in any year not to exceed the amount of interest
together with £100 of capital. The directions accom-

panying the bequest are liberal and sensible. It is to
be applied towards filling up deficiencies in theology, history, and literature. As to the
first class no books are to be included "which
treat on dogmatic or controversial subjects in a
spirit other than that of the scientific and unpreju-
diced pursuit of truth, and frank declaration of the
results from time to time attained by honest intellectual research, free from the bonds alike of
authority and preconception." There is no bar to
the purchase of valuable editions, "but not copies
having merely a bibliomaniacal value." The fund,
it is further to be noticed, is not intended to relieve
the college of any part of its usual expenditure on
the library. It will be interesting in the future to
notice what literature is placed on the college
shelves by this bequest, liberal alike in its pecuniary
extent and in the uses to which it is devoted.

The Owens College Library is, of course, intended
mainly for the use of those connected with the
college either as teachers or pupils; but outsiders
are allowed to avail themselves of its treasures on
application, properly recommended, to the Principal.
And the entire management of the institution is a
guarantee that no one is likely to be turned away
who can make good use of them.

IV.

SALFORD FREE LIBRARIES.

Our district has been honourably distinguished by its pioneer work in the provision of libraries really as well as nominally "public." The Chetham Library was the first in Europe that opened its doors to all comers; Manchester was the first town to avail itself of the facilities afforded by the Free Libraries Act of 1851, and the Salford Library was established just before that act was forced through Parliament against the opposition of Colonel Sibthorp and other shining intellectual lights.

The virtual founder of the Salford Library was the late Joseph Brotherton, one of those strongly marked characters who find their most congenial soil in the "north countrie." A vegetarian and teetotaller from religious motives, he was listened to with equal respect on the floor of the House of Commons and in the pulpit of his own chapel. Whilst the Committee on Public Libraries was receiving evidence the thought seems to have occurred to him of taking advantage of a clause in the Museums Act of 1845 to show that libraries would be duly appreciated and properly used if they were made accessible. To this happy inspiration Salford owes its system of free libraries. They now contain 53,624 volumes, the Greengate branch having 8,449, and that at Regent Road 7,537; the lion's share, of course, remaining with the parent institution at Peel Park, where the lending and reference departments contain 37,778 volumes. Of these not less than 23,996 have been presented to the institution, a circumstance creditable to the liberality of its friends. The average price paid for books, including those bought by public subscription at the commencement, has not exceeded two shillings per volume.

The proximity of the Reference Library to the Museum has not been without its influences. The scientific portions of the library—those in which it can most fittingly supplement and illustrate the Museum cases—are the strongest and the completest. The mere bookworm will not find here much to interest him. There are no MSS., no "Caxton's unique nor Wynkyn's uncut." There is one specimen of the workmanship of the latter, the Chronicles of Engelonde, printed in 1520. Its partial defects have been carefully supplied in writing by one whose soul "has been with the saints, we trust," for some centuries. There are a few old Bibles— the irrepressible "Breeches" edition, and the "Bishops" of 1583 being amongst them. Skene's Laws of Scotland (1597) is an interesting exemplar of Waldegrave's press, and has a philological interest from the "guid braid Scots" diction in which the law is laid down. The Bodoni edition of Tasso's Aminta should be inspected by those who delight in beautiful printing. What more delightful compilation of travels has ever been written than by Samuel Purchas, whose "Pilgrimages," the first part (1613) is here? Several of Mr. Halliwell's publications are in the library. In some instances only twenty-five copies were printed, and it is therefore specially important that they should be in public libraries. The "Book about Shakspere," Lodge's Margarite of America, and the reprints of jest books and tracts of the sixteenth and seventeeth centuries have all a literary as well as a bibliomaniacal interest. The "Birth and Triumph of Love" (1796) is the title of a choicely-printed but not otherwise lovely poem, written by Sir J. B. Burgess, and illustrated with some charming engravings, the designs apparently copied from Wedgwood's Queen's Ware. Another literary curiosity is a copy of Christopher Weigel's book of plates illustrating the different civil, religious, and military orders of the world. The work is most comprehensive, and ranges from the knights of the Round Table to the members of an equally mythical order of chivalry amongst the Florida Indians. Monks, hermits, begging friars, nuns, members of every association that religion or fanaticism could inspire, pass before one as in a long procession. The text is in manuscript, and has evidently been written in some Italian convent. Although finely written, yet, comparing this with the literary work of the monks of old, there is indeed a falling off—Hyperion to a Satyr.

In history and topography the collection is fairly supplied—Grose's Antiquities, Chauncey's Hertfordshire, a large paper copy of Ormerod's Cheshire, Dugdale's Monasticon, being of the number. The important Monumenta Historica Britannica is here, and a fine edition of Wyntoun's Chronicles. Amongst the archæological books we were glad to see Montfaucon's Antiquité Expliquée (1719), and the Vetusta Monumenta. The latter, if by no means all sterling gold, is yet a mine of good matter to dig in. A fit companion to it is the Archæologia, also published by the Society of Antiquaries, but unfortunately not complete. Here we may name the publications of the Chester Archæological, the Arundel, the Parker, the Hanserd Knollys, and other societies, possessing in varied degrees interest to the student of the past. Closely connected with the preceding are books descriptive of museums. The French edition of Gargiulio's Raccolta is little known, and contains good outline engravings of the choicest objects in the Neapolitan Museo Borbonico, which will now have dropped that unpopular name. More amusing, if less valuable, is a small folio about the Museo Moscardo (Verona, 1672), a private collection which had some strange objects in it. Giants' teeth are figured in one of the cuts, and unbelievers are silenced by a reference to Goliath. They are mammoth bones. Another wonder of this old museum was a stick of Indian ink! The British Museum was not much better. In Rymsdyk's account there is a notice of the Scythian Lamb, which was supposed to grow upon a tree. A coat, made from the wool of this creature, used to be one of the greatest treasures of the Bodleian Library at Oxford. It is really a tree-fern, which, in certain positions, a vivid imagination might suppose to resemble a lamb.

The books on numismatics are somewhat numerous. Perhaps the finest is that of Pedrusi on the medals of the Cæsars. Not even the coins of China have been forgotten in this section.

The local collections, if not very extensive, are interesting. The greater part of these have already

been described by the late Mr. John Harland, F.S.A.
A volume of odd numbers of old Manchester newspapers—one of them published in 1736—are amusing by contrast with the broadsheets of to-day. A
similar scrap-book is filled with political squibs and
ballads of the early part of this century, and another
relates to the Musical Festival. The (printed) deposi-
tions taken in connection with the trial of the
Fenians in 1867 make a curious volume. Relating to
an earlier period of political agitation and trouble
are a series of journals of which Wooler's Black
Dwarf may be taken as the type.

The lover of natural history will find much to
delight him in this library. The magnificent works
of Gould on the birds of Europe and Australia, and
the fauna of India have a beauty which beggars
description. There are also Bonaparte's Icono-
grafia della Fauna Italica (Roma 1837-41);
Reeve's Conchologia Iconica; the old coloured
Buffon, and many other costly works in illustration
of different portions of nature. One of these is an
interesting specimen of nature-printing executed at
Madras in the fatal year 1857. It is a folio of
impressions executed by Mr. Henry Smith, direct
from the leaves of unprepared plants.

The Salford Library possesses a fine collection of
parliamentary papers. Comparatively few are aware
of the importance of these publications. They are
indispensable to those who are studying the social
questions of the day; they give the fullest light on
the commerce and industry of foreign countries, and
sometimes contain matter which the antiquary and
the savant can hardly afford to neglect.

In estimating the Salford library, the most notable thing about it is its utilitarian character. It has been designed above everything else for work, and this, with its pronounced scientific direction, should make it specially useful, now that the claims and the importance of scientific culture are being so strongly insisted upon. The greatest defect is that of a printed catalogue, a want which, we may hope, its energetic curator and librarian, Mr. John Plant, F.G.S., will have supplied, along with the other benefits to be conferred upon the public by the extensions of the museum now in progress or in contemplation.

V.

THE ATHENÆUM.

The Manchester Athenæum is a huge club, offering many advantages at a very trifling cost, and adding to its social uses certain facilities for culture which the "swell" clubs do not possess. It will be in the memory of most of our readers that the library suffered by fire in September, 1873. Of its 20,000 volumes not one-half were found available for future use. Hence the library is intensely new, and has a certain interest as indicating the wants and tastes of the day, for the directors of a popular institution must consult the literary feeling of their constituents. The total number of volumes at present is upwards of thirteen thousand, and additions to the store are being made rapidly every week.

The strongest department, except perhaps the collection of Fiction, is that of English periodical literature. It was said of a recent writer, not unknown to the Manchester Athenæum, that he was writing plays at a time when the perusal of some odd volumes of old quarterly reviews would have been a wholesome mental discipline. It is painful to think of the intellectual wealth buried in old files of periodicals. In these days of condensation, he who would in a past age have written a book is contented or constrained to compress his thoughts into an article. This is so far a gain to both author and reader; the pity is that when the periodical is transferred from the table to the shelves it so seldom receives attention. Some of the writings of

our finest modern essayists—of Hunt, Hazlitt, De
Quincy, Carlyle, and many others—lie thus buried.
There are here long sets, in some cases complete, in
others approximating, of the Annual Register,
Athenæum, Gentleman's, Fraser, Cornhill, Hood,
Jerrold, and the Dublin University Magazine, the
Edinburgh, Westminster, Quarterly, and Dublin
Reviews; files of the Economist, the Saturday
Review, the British Almanac from the commence-
ment, and of the Times and Manchester Guardian
from 1836. To delight the lovers of old books,
there are sets of the Retrospective Review and Notes
and Queries.

The scientific and artistic sections include writings
of Ruskin and Pugin, and a fine series of works on
natural history presented by Mr. Mendel. The lover
of nature will be delighted with the pictorial
wealth of such books as Bree's Birds, Couch's
Fishes, Lowe's Ferns and Plants, and Pratt's
Flowering Plants. The Record of the United
States Exploring Expedition commanded by Wilkes
is as important to the scientific man as it is interesting to that omnivorous creature the "general
reader." It is a frequent complaint that the
English public do not buy or read the works of
original thinkers, and that scientific books which do
not aim at popularising what is already known, but
endeavour to add thereto, receive very scant encouragement. It is therefore worth noting that the
Athenæum possesses all the works of Mr. Herbert
Spencer—and that they are read. There is a good
array of English authors varying in date and
calibre more than Hobbes and Hone; portions of

Publications of the Camden, the Percy, the Old Shakspere, and the Manchester Literary and Philosophical Societies. There are Bohn's "cribs," dictionaries varying from Facciolati to Dr. William Smith, and encyclopædias from the old Penny to the last volume of the new issue of the Britannica.

Amongst the historical books is the fine work of Sir Samuel Meyrick on ancient armour, and that vast storehouse of English history known as Thurloe's State Papers. Stuart's Caledonia Romana should be interesting to the antiquaries of North Britain. Maimburg's Crusades is still curious, though now to a large extent superseded. For their interest to the antiquary we may name Ellesmere's Northern Archæology, Beltz's Order of the Garter, Blaauw's Barons' Wars, and Thorpe's Northern Mythology, although they vary greatly in value. There is an extensive series of modern works on biography. Amongst these we may specify Wright's Biographia Literaria, and Folsom's Hernando Cortez.

The local books include Baines, Gregson, Aikin, and Whitaker. There is also the Cheshire History of Ormerod, and the thick prospectus of its projected predecessor by Dr. Gower. The Albums issued in connection with the Athenæum are interesting little volumes, and amongst the pamphlets we may name one small tract by the late Archibald Prentice, giving some recollections of Jeremy Bentham.

The bibliographical works are not very numerous, but include several of Dibdin's books, Allibone's Dictionary, Brydge's Restituta, and Beloe's Anecdotes. There is a copy of the rare and interesting

Diary of a Lover of Literature, by Thomas Green; and of Dunton's Young Student's Library, published in 1692 by that versatile and vacillating character. We may name here Lubbock's important Essay on Classification, as dealing with a subject of great practical importance in every library of any size. There are few students of Chinese in Manchester, but the translation of Æsop into that language, with notes by Robert Thom, printed at Canton in 1841, is a literary curiosity.

It is intended to pay some attention to foreign literature in the future. This is a wise step, especially in view of the language classes of the institution. The young man who learns Spanish for the sake of its commercial uses may thus be tempted into the companionship of Cervantes and Lope. The nucleus of a collection of French, German, and Spanish literature is now being laid, and we hope that the acorn may hereafter grow into an oak. We may perhaps hint that the language of Dante is worthy of attention, and that Petrarch is at least not inferior to Yriarte.

Amongst the miscellaneous books we must be content to name only John Buncle, the "English Rabelais;" the long-withheld correspondence of Burns and Clarinda; the Lispings from Low Latitudes of the "Hon. Impulsia Gushington," and the very curious collection of Arabic Proverbs by John Lewis Burckhardt.

VI.

THE MECHANICS' INSTITUTION.

The library of the Mechanics' Institution contains about 14,000 volumes. In 1873 it issued 27,242 volumes to the members; in 1874 22,353, a considerable decrease. Looking to quality we find that 14,356 of the last named were works of fiction, 42 related to finance, and 147 to theology—a puzzling proportion, for in Manchester we are credited with a strong desire to master the money-making art, and judged to be somewhat careless on religious matters. Those who are afraid of the luxury of the age will be glad to learn that 258 volumes on economy were read, or at least borrowed. We have a very modified faith as to the value of returns of this sort, as there are usually local causes at work, which determine the class of books read. The high proportion borne by fiction to the other departments of literature is probably due to the healthy delight which schoolboys take in Ivanhoe and Redstocking.

It would not be wise to expect a large proportion of rare or curious books in a library of this character designed, as its name implies, for a class who are not usually distinguished by bibliomaniac ardour, however much they may be imbued with a love of literature. Still it has some fine books. Following the catalogue classification, in history we may name the Archæologia Scotica, Howard on Prisons (1780), Christopher Wordsworth's Inscriptiones Pompeianæ, and Stuart and Revett's fine folios on the Antiquities of Athens.

There is an old folio of Holinshed, but it is unfortunately incomplete. This chronicler was the fountain from which Shakspere is believed to have drawn much of his historical matter.

Considerable attention has been paid to local history, and the library contains the " Foundations of Manchester," and works bearing on the subject by Catt, Palmer, Procter, Reilly, Whitaker, Aikin, Baines, Bancks Everett, Gregson, Wheeler, and others. The rarest and now probably the most interesting is a volume of Views of Ancient Buildings by Jackson, in 1823, when Manchester had not yet been shorn of almost every relic of antiquity. Here we may name the Gazettes issued in connection with the institution itself. Dudley's Tree of Commonwealth may in a sense be termed a local book, since, although written by its author in the reign of Henry VIII., in prison and under sentence of death, it remained in manuscript 250 years, when a few copies were printed for the Brotherhood of the Rosy Cross, and edited by the late John Harland. The original edition of Lowe's Description of Manchester in 1783, is most carefully preserved, according to the desire of its donor.

The biographical section offers good reading, though it presents some odd points, as in possessing two volumes of Rousseau's Correspondence, and not having the " Confessions" at all.

The books in geography and travels include Lord F. Egerton's Mediterranean Sketches, Phillipps' Views of the Old Halls of Lancashire, and some hundreds of well-known tales of travellers in every clime.

The scientific section is that on which apparently the greatest care has been expended. It is extensive, and contains the cream of the more popular scientific works published in the last generation.

Clarke's Menai Bridge, Rawlinson's Designs for Tall Chimney Shafts, Stevenson's Bell Rock Lighthouse, and Smeaton's Eddystone Lighthouse will interest some, whilst Smethurst's Tables of Time may be named as an early specimen of Manchester printing.

Curtis's British Entomology is a finely illustrated work; its coloured plates will be very useful to the "butterfly hunters."

A quaint old book belonging to the geological ages of science is John Bate's Mysteries of Nature and Art, published in 1635.

The Rariores Plantæ Horti Farnesiani of T. A. Cesenate (Rome, 1625), is a rare and interesting botanical work. This copy was formerly in the British Museum, by whose authorities it was sold as a duplicate in 1787. The only MS. the institution possesses is of a scientific character—a folio of "Tables for ascertaining the number of Weft Threads in Twilled Goods," by Bennet Woodcroft, F.R.S., who was then resident in this neighbourhood, and presented this elaborate work to the library.

Social and Domestic Economy ranges from Quetelet on Man to the Finchley Cooking Manual; the class of mental and moral philosophy is almost equally wide ranging; and that of philology is chiefly composed of schoolbooks and "cribs" in political economy. We notice MacCulloch's bibliography of what has been ignorantly stigmatized as the dismal science.

The works of imagination in poetry and prose do not call for special notice, except to name the "Offering to Lancashire," edited by Miss Craig. This little volume of graceful verse is a memorial of goodwill for this district when it was under a cloud. The poets gave their verses, the women-printers gave their toil, the manufacturer presented the paper, in order that every shilling the public paid for the book might go to gladden the cottage homes of Lancashire in the days of the cotton famine.

Amongst the miscellaneous section are some of the earlier works on the temperance movement, notably the inquiry into the effect of fermented liquors by Basil Montagu.

Under the qeeer heading of Parliamentary Papers, &c. are included some local tracts of considerable interest.

The cyclopædias include the Britannica, Knight's, Partington's, and the Popular.

Amongst the periodicals are 108 volumes of the Critical Review, Taylor's Scientific Memoirs, the Westminster Review, New Monthly Magazine, &c. Some of the older popular science periodicals are here, such as Pinnock's Guide, the Polytechnic, Newton's Journal, &c., the Phrenological Journal, once of some importance, and the North of England Medical Journal, which in 1831 contained the contributions of our most eminent local medicine men.

Most libraries have acquired a habit of accepting whatever gifts are offered to them, asking no questions (for conscience sake?) as to their value.

It is thus that the foreign section of the library may be conjectured to have been supplied. It contains a few notable books; for instance, the Theatrum Machinarium Generale, of Leupold, 3 vols., folio (1724), with its quaint pictures of old-fashioned industries. The volume named "French pamphlets" in the catalogue are the production of Baron Charles Dupin, and bear his autograph inscription presenting them to the institution. In this section, too, we meet with the oldest book the library possesses—a copy of the Rudimenta Mathematica of Sebastian Munster, printed at Basle in 1551, and illustrated with some interesting woodcuts of clocks and other instruments for marking time. Munster is said to have been little but learned, and equally familiar with the interior of clocks and Hebrew books.

VII.

THE BIBLE CHRISTIAN CHURCH LIBRARY, SALFORD.

Most of the places of worship in this district have libraries connected with them. These church, chapel, and Sunday school libraries are no doubt doing excellent service, but for the most part they do not possess that literary importance which would necessitate their inclusion in the present series of papers. We may remark, in passing, that whilst serving their principal purpose of fostering the religious sentiment of the sects to which they belong they might be made of greater educational value, if more care were taken to include in them the masterpieces of our English literature, and greater stress were laid upon goodness and less upon the cheapness of the books added. Still, with all drawbacks, we believe the libraries of the religious communities are doing good, and one or two have special claims upon our attention. Of these perhaps the least known and the most interesting is that in connection with the Bible Christian Church in Cross Lane, Salford.

The Rev. William Cowherd, the founder of the sect of Bible Christians, was born at Carnforth, Lonsdale, south of the Sands, in 1763. He became a teacher of philology in a college at Beverley, intended for the preparation of candidates for the ministry. He came to Manchester and acted as curate to the Rev. John Clowes, M.A., and here became a student of the writings of Swedenborg.

He is said to be the only man who ever read through
all the Latin writings of the Swedish sage.   Mr.
Clowes, although holding the doctrine of the " New
Church," never saw any reason to leave the Anglican
communion, but after a while Mr. Cowherd gave up
his engagement at St. John's and preached for a
short time in the Swedenborgian temple in Peter-
street.   He left because he was not satisfied with the
hierarchical development of the sect, which did not
allow sufficient freedom of opinion for him.   In
1800 he built at his own expense Christ Church in
King-street, Salford, and his ability and earnestness
as a preacher soon attracted a large congregation.
The seats were free.   He held a view, now unpopular, that it was the duty of a minister to main-
tain himself, and therefore had an " Academy" or
school with accommodation for a considerable number of boarders.   In this enterprise he was assisted
by several gentlemen, who were afterwards ordained
by him for ministers.   Two of them, the Rev.
William Metcalfe and the Rev. J. Clarke, went to
Philadelphia.   The latter became a farmer, but the
former founded the Bible Christian Church, which
still flourishes in the city of brotherly love.   Metcalfe graduated M.D., and, in accordance with his
master's injunction, gained a living by the
practice of medicine.   During a temporary sojourn in
Manchester it was his lot to preach the funeral sermon of the late Joseph Brotherton.   The Rev. J.
Schofield, who built the Round Chapel in Every-
street, also practised medicine.   Cowherd built
Christ Church Institute, Hulme, where the Revs. J.
Clarke and Schofield (before he went to Every-street)

officiated. It came afterwards into the hands of the late James Gaskill, who, at his death, left an endowment for its continuance as an educational institution.

In 1809, Mr. Cowherd promulgated views which were a severe test of his popularity. The members of the Bible Christian Church pledged themselves to "eat no more meat while the world standeth." Intoxicating liquors were also placed under interdict. The motive of this was partly scientific and partly religious. Besides "keeping a school and calling it an academy," he dabbled in physic, and in the latter part of his iife was best known as, Dr. Cowherd. The medical arguments of Cheyne, and the humanitarian sentiments of St. Pierre, probably gave rise to a system of life which he held to have "proof of Holy Writ." He died in 1816, and was buried in the graveyard in front of his chapel. His epitaph ends with the words, inscribed at his request, "All feared, none loved, few understood." This has often been thought to point to his personal history, and to indicate an unhappy life. Unhappy in some respects the life may perhaps have been, but the epitaph is simply adapted from the verses of Pope, who declares of those who wish

———————— to save a sinking land
All fear, none love, few understand.

One of his pupils, and who for forty years was engaged in the ministry of this church, was Joseph Brotherton, the first M.P. for Salford.

Cowherd was a man probably of imperious temper, but certainly of great intellectual force and literary culture.   A press was set up at the Academy, and after his death printed what is a lasting memorial of his wide reading and research. Under the somewhat fantastic title of "Facts Authentic in Science and Religion towards a new Translation of the Bible," he had collected matter illustrative of passages of Scripture and in defence of his own interpretation of them.   Travellers, lawyers, poets, physicians, all are pressed into service, the book forming really a portly quarto commonplace book, filled with reading as delightful as it is discursive.   Some of his minor writings have also been printed.   He was a practical chemist and astronomer, and had the dome of the church in King-street fitted up for the joint purpose of observatory and laboratory.   His microscope is still preserved at Peel Park Museum.   The Bible Christians have not yet made a new heaven and a new earth, but they have prospered to an extent that has rendered removal to a larger and more modern building desirable.   To the new Bible Christian Church in Cross Lane was removed, with other relics, the valuable library left for the use of the members by the founder William Cowherd. It was at one time a circulating library, accessible to the public on easy terms, but the books are not such as can be read by those who run. They bear the impress of the strong mind which brought them together for its own uses.   This library is the workshop in which he wrought out a new mode of life and a new theory of doctrine.   With these tools he moulded minds like that of Brotherton; and so his influence has worked in many unseen channels.

Put your hand casually upon these shelves, and

in half mocking sortilege draw forth a book. The
dii tutelares are watchful here: it is the fine edition
of Jamblichus, printed by Aldus in 1516! This is a
commencement that puts the book-lover on his
mettle. Nor will he be disappointed. The fullest
department is that of Theology. Here is a
good copy of Walton's Polyglot, but although
dated 1657 it has neither the dedication to
Oliver Cromwell, nor, that which superseded it,
to Charles II., but stands halting between two
opinions. Then we have Hutter's Bible (Hamburgh,
1587), and Poole's Synopsis Criticorum. Suiceri
Thesaurus Ecclesiasticus (Amsterdam, 1682) contains the autograph of Thomas Deacon, presumably
that of " the greatest of sinners and most unworthy
of primitive bishops," as his epitaph styles him. To
this class belongs a fine specimen of local enterprise.
It is an edition, in folio, of the Douay and Rheims
Bible, with notes selected by the Rev. George Leo
Haydock. It is enriched with twenty engravings,
apparently executed for the work, which must have
involved a large outlay on the part of Thomas
Haydock, by whom it was printed and published in
1811, at his " Catholic Publication Warehouse,
2, Stable-street, Lever's Row, Manchester." It is a
little puzzling to guess both where Haydock found pur-
chasers and what the buyers did with the book. The
present writer has examined many thousand volumes
without encountering a second copy of this book.
Then there is the volume of "Annotations" on
the Bible, " by the labour of certain divines" (third
edition, 1657). These Presbyterian lights were
slightingly said to have made very free with Dio-

dati's work, which they, as in duty bound, do stoutly deny. The antiquity of certain subjects is curiously shown in Dr. Robert Gell's "Essay toward the amendment of the last English translation of the Bible" (1659). Two centuries later, and the amendment has not yet come, though we may be on the eve of it. Even the most determined grumbler at the Authorised Version, if he compare it with the unidiomatic tameness of the Douay translation, will find enough to give him pause in his complaints. Let us hope that the Revisers will deal tenderly with this grand "well of English undefiled." Of another cast is one of Bishop Montagu's works, "Apparatvs ad Origines Ecclesiasticas. Collectore R. Montacvtio. Oxoniæ, 1635," folio.

As the founder of a Swedenborgian Church, we should expect to find a vein of mystic literature amongst Cowherd's books. Here are the "Works of the Teutonic Philosopher," Jacob Behmen, edited by the Rev. William Law in 1764. There are also some separate books of Behmen's, amongst others the very rare and interesting edition of his "Way to Life," printed in Manchester in 1752, not improbably at the instigation of John Byrom, who was a reader and admirer of the quaint German mystic. Swedenborg is here in strength. In a copy of the Arcana Cœlestia, Cowherd has written a note that on the western coast of Africa there were then existing two Oracles as famous and as sacred as that of Delphos. There are the works of Henry Cornelius Agrippa, the Commentary of Hierocles, printed by Urie at Glasgow (second edition, 1756), Porphyry (Lugdunii, 1620), and others.

Another class of mystics may serve to turn our attention to a notable feature in this library. From Van Helmont, on the Spirit of Diseases (1694), to Lambe's Additional Reports (1815) it is rich in the writings of those who have, sometimes with and sometimes without philosophic insight, treated medical and physiological questions from novel points of view. Amongst these we may name a series of the books written by Thomas Tryon, an English Pythagorean of the eighteenth century, who persisted in maintaining life and literary vigour on a regimen of herbs and fruits to the great amazement of his contemporaries. Whether "Philotheos Physiologus" (so did T. T. sometimes mask) tell us the Way to Health and Long Life, or hold forth on Cleanliness in Meats and Drinks, he is always amusing and sometimes instructive. Another entertaining work of the same class is that whose quaint title is here copied :—"Long Livers : a curious history . . . with the rare Secret of Rejuvenescy of Arnoldus de Villa Nova. By Eugenius Philalethes, F.R.S. London, 1722." Alas, Arnoldus is dust, and Eugenius Philalethes, F.R.S., is gone to his grave, and the method of renewing our youth like the eagle is a dead secret indeed. Hufeland's Art of prolonging Life and Pat. Delany's Doctrine of Abstinence from Blood may both be placed in this group, which also contains such works as Oswald's Cry of Nature (1791), and other advocacies of Vegetarianism.

Extensive and valuable as the library still is, it

does not represent the full extent of Cowherd's reading, for some portions have in past years been sold. The collection now is more valuable to the antiquary than to the student, but we hope it will always remain intact as a memento of a remarkable man. The tradition of earnestness and culture which has descended to his disciples will long ensure that his memory be thus honoured.

VIII.

LITERARY AND PHILOSOPHICAL SOCIETY

AND OTHER SCIENTIFIC ASSOCIATIONS.

The Manchester Literary and Philosophical Society won its spurs before the present century was born. Royalty gave it a cheap patronage, the names of Dalton, Ferriar, Eaton Hodgkinson, and Henry, and later of Joule, Schunck, Angus Smith, and Fairbairn, have spread its fame throughout Europe. This reputation has been of essential service in the construction of its library. The intrinsic value of the publications it can offer. has brought it in exchange .the works published by many of the most important of the learned societies of the world.* The collection is indeed almost exclusively restricted to this one department. It has no claim to be considered a general library of literature and science; it is not even a fair scientific collection, but in its own speciality it is unsurpassed in the district, and there are very few that can compete with it in the kingdom. This speciality, as already indicated, is in the transactions, memoirs, and journals which preserve the results obtained by those who are engaged in laboriously extending the boundaries of

---

* The important position taken by the Society is shown by the German translation of the early volumes of its memoirs:—" Physikalische und Philosophische Abhandlungen der Gesellschaft der Wissenschaften zu Manchester. Leipzig, 1788."

knowledge. The activity with which this process is carried on is simply amazing. As a fitting memorial of the long labours of the late Dr. John Edward Gray, of the British Museum, a list of his writings was published soon after his death. The number of distinct entries in it, including books, pamphlets, and articles in magazines and publications of societies, amounted to close upon 1,200. It is not every student who is so keen an observer, or who has taken so thoroughly to heart the advice of Captain Cuttle, but still the life of the *naturforscher* affords very many opportunities for adding new facts to those already recorded. In this respect the students of science have an advantage over those who engage in the pursuits of literature. The collection of facts, however humble a task, has its uses, and these are duly recognised. In going over a long series of transactions, the bulk of the papers will be found to be chiefly records of patient and accurate investigation. These at rare intervals serve as the foundation for the generalizations of some master who shows their correlation, and wrests from them a knowledge of the laws underlying them.

One of the wants of the English language is a common term adequately describing the associations, animated it is true by the same spirit, but widely diverse in their aims and operations, which we call learned societies. The term academy, so conveniently restricted to them by Continental usage, is in England only at the present moment in the process of being rescued from the hands of schoolmasters. The academies are the creation of the Renaissance, though there are not wanting occasional traces of similar institutions of earlier date, and the name suggests the golden grove where Plato taught. The fanciful genius of Italy ran riot in her academies, even the names suggesting the exuberance of a new-found delight. Thus we have such conceits as styling a scientific society the Academy of the Lynxes. The publications of this society are to be found here, and of the many notable associations which have succeeded it. The Accademia del Cimento was one of the very earliest for the investigation of physical science. It flourished under royal patronage, had great men amongst its members, and owned no law but that of the duty of truth-seeking. The "Essayes of Natural Experiments" made in it were published by its secretary, and are here in an English translation (London, 1684) by Richard Waring, F.R.S. The Italian academies have often a literary flavour appertaining even to their severest studies. The Academy of Science, Literature, and Art, of Lucca, indulges in a characteristic outbreak on occasion of the marriage of the Archduke Ferdinand with the Princess Anna Maria of Saxony. It is a common custom in Italy amongst the wealthier classes to print memorial volumes for distribution at weddings. These are sometimes reprints of old books or documents connected with the family history of one or other of the happy pair, and sometimes simply the congratulation of friendly rhymers. The academy made up an album (printed in the same volume with antiquarian and botanical papers) expressive of their "exultation" at the royal marriage. The secretary opens with a sonnet, but it is immediately eclipsed by some Hebrew verses, to which the author has mercifully appended a translation; then follows an epigram in Greek and Latin, and various Italian poems and epigraphs. There is something comical in the spectacle of a band of greybeards filling twenty-seven pages with this kind of thing.

We are not objecting to the union of literature and science; on the contrary, we hold it is a grievous loss to culture that they should be pursued on diverse lines. It cannot be too often recalled to memory that all knowledge is one; that our distinctions are simply arbitrary conveniences, and that new discoveries very commonly arise from new combination of old principles and facts. Hence one great advantage of the prosecution of diverse studies in one society. The Royal Society, when its existence commenced, was intended for the "improvement of natural knowledge," the word natural being used not as equivalent to physical but to exclude subjects belonging to the domain of theology or supernatural knowledge. It embraced all the fields of secular learning then cultivated, and it is to be regretted that gradually its scope has become more limited, and independent societies have arisen to deal with special branches. No one looks now for archæological matter in the Philosophical Transactions; it has to be sought for in the publications of the various antiquarian societies, and the same remark applies with more or less force to many other subjects. "It would be a great assistance of the history of science," says Mr. Weld, "if the Philosophical Transactions contained, as in former times, the first account of philosophical discoveries."

The history of the French Institute exhibits the converse result. The union of independent academies has there, without destroying their individuality, resulted in a powerful institution " where all the efforts of the human mind are bound together in one sheaf." The founders of the Literary and Philosophical Society of Manchester, judging from its name, must have intended to organize a union of literature and science, but literature has long since been dropped out of its programme.

The library contains the publications, in some cases incomplete, of the Academies of Utrecht, Berlin, Munich, Prague, Helsingfors, Upsal, Bordeaux, Milan, Vienna, Pesth, Mans, Rochelle, Nantes, Brussels, Haarlem, Catania, Lucca, Naples, Palermo, Venice, Leipzig, Leyden, Algiers, Auxerre, Geneva, Neuchâtel, St. Petersburg, Strassburg, Lisbon, Christiania, Stockholm, Paris, Frankfurt, Madras, Kazan, Abbeville, Dijon, Liege, Lille, Lyon, Metz, Montpellier, Nancy, Nîmes, Madrid, Bologna, Amsterdam, Altenburg, Göttingen, Batavia, Copenhagen, Rouen, Luxembourg, Kiel, Trondheim, Rheims, and many others. The chief English societies are well represented The early volumes of the Philosophical Transactions are here only in an abridged form, but its later issues are complete; and supplemented by the records of the Royal Society of Edinburgh, the Royal Irish Academy, the Society of Antiquaries, and most of the other leading scientific associations.

The Oriental department seems fairly well filled, having the Oriental Translation Fund books and the publications of the Asiatic Societies of London,

Bengal, Bombay, and Batavia, but being deficient in the important works of the German, French, Italian, and American societies devoting themselves to the same subject. Anthropology is very poorly represented. Generally speaking, the strength of the library corresponds with the recent development of the Society, which has been mainly in the direction of the physical sciences. Thus we find here the American Philosophical Society, and the Academy of Sciences of America, but not its Social Science Association, nor its numerous associations for the study of literature and antiquities. The valuable books of the Smithsonian Institution should be named.

The library has been twice catalogued, the last one being issued in the present year :—

Catalogue of the Books in the Library of the Manchester Literary and Philosophical Society. Francis Nicholson, Hon. Librarian. Manchester: T. Sowler, 1875, 8vo, pp. 173.

The classification adopted is: General Science; Chemistry; Pharmacy; Statistics; Geography and Travels; Optics, Hydraulics, and Dynamics; Microscopical; Photography; History and Biography; Engineering; Agriculture; Catalogues; Architecture and Archæology; Astronomy; Meteorology; Magnetism and Electricity; Patents; Natural History; Botany; Geology; Mathematics; and Miscellaneous. The last class ranges from the texts of the classics published by Mai from the Vatican codices to a MS. glossary of the Lancashire Dialect by Samuel Bamford, and includes alike Dalton's English Grammar and Marshman's translation of Confucius. It also contains a goodly number of uncatalogued pamphlets. The catalogue shows unfortunately that several of the works want sundry volumes to make them complete. It shows also that whilst the Society possesses a fine collection of books, it is one that stands in need of considerable strengthening in several departments.

The general public have only a very faint conception of the variety and interest that lies locked up in the "Transactions" of societies. With the exception of parliamentary papers there is perhaps no class of printed matter so little read. Even professed students and bibliographers here neglect much that would delight them. This is mainly due to the absence of any general guide to their contents. A library made up of such materials is indeed a mighty maze without a plan. The title does not assure the mathematician that he will find something germane to his studies in the Atalantis of the Catholic University of Ireland, and the philologist cannot feel certain that the Mémoires of the St. Petersburg Academy will reward his labours. The Royal Society have in hand a Catalogue of Scientific Papers from 1800 to 1860, but this does not include literary, archæological, or professional papers—a fact greatly diminishing its value. The inquirer is still therefore practically left to his own guidance; but if he have patience and intelligence he will reap a rich reward.

Amongst the non-biblical matters we should name the memorials of Dalton, Eaton Hodgkinson, Dr. Henry, and Dr. Percival. The philosophical instruments of Dalton are still carefully preserved. A late addition is a bust of James Wolfenden, a self-taught mathematician, who died on the verge of starvation.

Some of the other Manchester societies possess libraries, but they do not call for extended notice. The Geological Society has a capital collection of books on that science, including much of interest and importance bearing on Palæontology and the antiquity of man. A list of these has been printed:

Catalogue of the Library of the Manchester Geological Society. Edited by John Plant, F.G.S. February, 1875. 8vo., pp. 38. Salford : J. Roberts.

The Statistical, Photographic, and Scientific and Mechanical Societies, and the Scientific Students' Association possess collections of books which may serve hereafter for the foundation of serviceable libraries.

IX.

THE MEDICAL.

The Medical Library of Manchester is considered to be the best in England outside London. It is the property of the Manchester Medical Society, which was originally founded in 1834, and after an existence marked by the fluctuations of fortune which wait on most organizations, was for a number of years identified with the Royal Institution. It has quite recently made an arrangement, mutually advantageous, with the authorities of Owens College. There, we may hope, it will continue to find a permanent home. The work of the society is " the promotion of medical science by the maintenance of a library and reading-room, and by the holding of meetings for reading papers and discussing subjects relating to that science."

The library contains about 16,000 volumes and in its new abode has space to grow to twice its present size. The actual extent of the library is much greater than these numbers would imply. There exists in medical literature a body of monographs on special subjects which, although complete treatises, do not exceed in size a bulky pamphlet. In past years, at least, it has been usual to bind a number of these together in one volume The actual number of entries in the catalogue will probably exceed 25,000. One cause which has proved very efficacious in producing a great quantity of medical monographs has not been equally operative as to quality. The regulations of many universities require the candidate to present a dissertation before a degree is conferred. Custom has led to the printing of these. The youthful aspirant is no doubt in many cases delighted to see his work in print and to give the copies away to his friends. The Advocates' Library at Edinburgh is said to possess over a hundred thousand of such exercises of ingenuous youth. These dissertations are sometimes interesting, as showing the early bent of great minds. Even when they do not contain a single original thought or fresh experiment they indicate the level of the tide of medical knowledge in the homes of general learning at the time when they were compiled.

There is a printed list of authors and an index of subjects in manuscript for reference :

Alphabetical Catalogue of the Library of the Manchester Medical Society. Prepared by John Roberts, M.D., hon. librarian. Manchester. 1866. 8vo., pp. 462.

Supplementary Catalogue. Prepared by C. Currie Ritchie, M.D., hon. librarian. Manchester. 1872. pp. 310.

The library has been exceedingly well built up. One result is the general harmonious proportion of the different classes. In some libraries one department will resemble Daniel Lambert and another will be as spare as Claude Seurat, the " living skeleton." It is, however, stronger in German than in French, and, what is remarkable in an English library, it contains a good number of Dutch books. Of Spanish, on the contrary, old or modern, there are very few.

There are many finely illustrated works. They are not of the kind usually left on drawing-room tables, and, despite the skill which many of them display, lovers of the fine arts are not likely to patronize them largely. Some of the anatomical works would be useful to painters as well as to physicians. Poor Haydon tells how as a youth he used to study his Albinus, lying at full length with the book open before him on the floor. His eyes would have glistened at some of the fine works here. We may name for examples the copy of the Anatomy of Bourgery and Jacob, eight folio volumes of coloured plates; the work on topographical anatomy of Paulet and Sarazin; Vicq d'Azyr's fine plates on the brain; the Anatomy of Caldani, extending to four large folio volumes of plates, and the same number in quarto of text; Rayer's work on the diseases of the kidneys, with coloured plates; and many more than we can now name. One of the most curious is Vrolik's "Tabulæ," from which a painter might glean figures for the grotesque horrors of a Walpurgis night. Here, too, the student may examine the progress of art and science by a comparison of Bartisch (1686 not first edition) on the diseases of the eye, and its modern successor, Dalrymple (1852). The fine plates of the old book, spirited as they are, must yield before the careful drawing and accurate colouring of the last named. We will pass from this class by naming Sandifort's catalogue of the Anatomical Museum of the Leyden Academy, an immense work which was some forty years in publication.

Fathers of the medical art are well represented. Thus of the works of Hippocrates there are a dozen editions, amongst them that of 1526, that of Mack

(1743), the French by Dacier (1697), the later one by Littré, the German by Grimm, and many more. This is without counting the editions of separate works, which are numerous. A very choice one is that edited by J. B. Lefebvre, and printed at Constantinople in 1782. The best edition of the "Opera" is that edited by Dr. F. G. Ermerins. A number of works from the valuable collection made by him in the course of his researches in classical medicine are in the library. His other editions of the classics are here. Of Dioscorides there are amongst others the Aldine edition, and the earlier one of Paris. We may notice here the sumptuous edition of Oribasius, that came from the French Imperial Printing Press in 1858, under the editorial care of Bussemaker and Daremberg. Of Celsus there are various editions, ranging from 1528 downwards. That issued at Naples by Salvatore de Renzi is so perfect that it is unlikely a new one will be attempted. The learned editor has given the text, with an Italian translation, bibliography, glossary, and critical apparatus for its understanding. The woodcuts of medical instruments are given from those found in Pompeii and Herculaneum. This is not the only good work of De Renzi. He is the author of a history of medical science in Italy, and of the "Collectio Salernitana," relating to the famous school of Salerno. Of Rhazes there is the Arabic and Latin edition printed by Bowyer.

There is a curious volume, "De Cirogia,"—an Italian translation of Gui de Chauliac, printed at Venice in 1480 (folio). The translator is careful to tell us that he has translated it word for word to

H

the glory of God.   Although the form may be
grotesque, a little more of the spirit would be no
unwelcome addition to the work of our own day.
Amongst other early works we may name the best
edition of Arnold de Villanova (Basel, 1585, fol.)
and the "Conciliator" of Petrus de Abano (1496.)
The "Practica ' of Michele Savonarola (Venet., 1497)
is interesting from his relationship to the great
owner of that high-sounding but lowly-meaning
surname.   There are several of the books printed by
the Junta amongst them the collection of treatises
on Baths, issued in 1553.

Braunschweigh's "Chirurgia," printed at Augsburg
in 1539, is an interesting work, perhaps the earliest
practical surgical book in the German language.
The wood engravings are roughly done, but sometimes effective, and the drawings not deficient in
spirit.   Far ruder are the illustrations of the German
"Hortus Sanitatus," printed at Strassburg in 1536.
It is full of woodcuts of possible and impossible
monsters, ranging from dragons to those nameless
pests which are especially fond of such habitats as
the bedrooms of seaside lodging-houses.   One of the
woodcuts represents a gentle insecticide trying to
brush out some similar but smaller nuisances from
the head of a male relative.   The head is extended
over a capacious bucket, suggestive of coming
woe to vast numbers of the insect tribe.   The
Bombast of Hohenheim is here, as a matter of course.
The vast but confused genius of Paracelsus has left
its impress on medical history.   The library contains not only the Latin edition of his works (1658),
but the German Strassburg edition, which includes

the explanation of the Magic Figures in the Nuremburg Cloister omitted in the other. The works of another strange genius—Cardan—extend to ten folio volumes.

In periodical literature the library is rich. This must necessarily be the case in a collection reflecting the history and progress of medical science. Not only are there here the leading English periodicals, but long sets of Virchow's Archiv, and similar journals.

Medical bibliography is of great importance. The lists given in the encyclopædias of that science are, as a matter of course, far from covering the entire ground. Various attempts at a book-list of medical science have been made, one of the latest is that of Pauly—"Bibliographie des Sciences Medicales." Paris. 1872. Bibliography is taking vigorous root in America. The old world will have to look to its laurels in this respect. Such a work as the bibliography of cholera, by Dr. J. S. Billings, included in Woodworth's Report on the Cholera Epidemic of 1873, reflects high credit upon the compiler. The new world does not yet offer the same facilities for the student, but on the other hand the very mass of literature contained in the great European libraries may have a disheartening effect.

An important American work, published under the auspices of the Government, is a Medical History of the War of the Rebellion, 1861-65. Various transactions of American medical societies are here, containing much that is interesting but very unequal in value. We may remark that many of the medical societies in the United States are subsidized to a certain extent by the States in which they exist. Hence they are able to issue large and sometimes luxurious volumes of transactions. This facility of printing has, however, led to the neglect of the noble art, "to blot." The faculty of saying in a hundred words that which ought to be said in ten is not a form of human ingenuity deserving of much encouragement.

The library contains a good number of works on the history of medicine, and, as will be seen by some of the titles we have enumerated, it contains a good deal that would help a new investigation of that interesting subject. It is perhaps under this head we can most fittingly name the photographic albums of portraits of medical men, presented to the library by Dr. Samelson.

The library has been chiefly formed by the care and energy of Mr. Thomas Windsor, and shows his widereaching knowledge of medical literature.

X.

THE EXCHANGE SUBSCRIPTION LIBRARY.

The Manchester Royal Exchange Subscription Library has undergone some curious transitions of locality and fortune. Established in troublous times, when there was no particular desire on the part of the authorities that knowledge should be increased, it was first known as the "Manchester Reading Society," afterwards as the "Manchester New Circulating Library," then as the Manchester Subscription Library, Exchange-street, and finally it adopted its present designation. The preliminary meeting was held August 29th, 1792, at 10, Broome-street, Shudehill. The name of Mr. Joseph Priestley (the son of the celebrated Birmingham philosopher) is the first on the list of members. It is not improbable that he interested his father in the scheme, for at the fourth meeting (September 4) a letter was read from Joseph Priestley, either the doctor or his son, asking their acceptance of eighty-five volumes of books. These probably formed the nucleus of the present collection. The books are varied in character. The first is Cook's Voyages, in four volumes; there are various works of Priestley's, some of Paine's political writings, and books and pamphlets relating to the Unitarian controversy and to the political disputes of the time. Priestley's name

was not one in very great favour with the ruling
powers, and the admission of his writings, coupled
with those of Paine, seems to have led to the institution being stigmatized as the "Jacobin Library."
It was found necessary to contradict by public
advertisement statements that the library was
intended for the diffusion of "seditious views."
The committee further resolved that the librarian
should be "directed immediately to remove out of
the library any book which *may happen* to be
deemed libellous." It was rumoured in the August
of 1793 that Mr. Thomas Butterworth Bayley, the
well-known chairman of the Salford Quarter
Sessions, was coming to seize anything he could
find there libellous or seditious. It must be confessed
that, had such a domiciliary visit been paid during
the early years of the library's existence, some of
the books would have been in danger of an
auto-da-fé. The committee of the Jacobin Library
had apparently adopted the then novel plan of
hearing both sides of the question. They bought
Wakefield's answer to Paine's Age of Reason,
but they bought the book attacked as well. The
Encyclopædia Britannica could only be purchased
by a special subscription amongst the members.
The original charge was not to exceed six shillings
per annum, the price of the share or ticket being
half-a-crown to the foundation members and five
shillings to those who joined later.

When John Stanley Gregson was portraying with
humorous talent the Manchester men and manners
of 1823, the radical tendencies of the Subscription
Library had apparently vanished, and it was a

fashionable lounge. He is satirical on "silly mothers." These—

> Creatures, devoid of taste for mental food,
> Send here for picture-books to please their brood.
>
> . . . . .
>
> Witness the *Sports and Pastimes of the East,*
> By thousand buttered thumbs and fingers greas'd,
> And *Forbes's Memoirs,* rich with many a plate,
> Conn'd o'er by readers rising three feet eight;
> Its flowers, its fruits, its birds of plumage bright,
> Tigers, snakes, lizards, touched without affright.

He also sketches the blue-stockings of the period, taking off their "thin kid shoes" to warm their feet by the fire, whilst they have a socal chat on Shakpere and the musical glasses.

> Scanning a catalogue, one now begins:—
> " My dear Letitia, give me, love, two pins;
> *Highways and Byeways; Tales pick'd up in France.*
> Last night I went to Mrs. Sprightly s dance.
> The *Flood of Thessaly* is quite divine;
> The cakes were musty, and how poor the wine!
> Miss Careful tore her Esterhazy frock;
> What are the *Memoirs of* this *Captain Rock?*
> Who is the author?" "*Not* himself, 'tis said."
> "Oh, no, my dear, 'tis Thomas Moore, instead,"
> "Oh, la! it must be good. I'll have the book,"
> P'rhaps 'tis like Hafed in his *Lalla Rookh.*
> Is *Captain Rock* at home?" "No, he's gone out."
> "I will not go to Mrs. Riot's rout;
> Where shall I seek Moore's *Odes,* or *Angel's Love?*"
> "One's at your feet, the other high above."
> "Here's Fletcher's *Trial, Court of Common Sense;*
> I bought some gloves at Lloyd's for fifteen pence;
> And as I paced along the well-fill'd Square,
> You cannot think how gentlemen did stare.

Well, my dear Jane, I know not what to take;
Here's Herbert's *Helga* and James Hogg's *Queen's Wake*.
Have you read either?   Really, I must go;
Ask for *Don Juan*, love, but whisper low."
" Priscilla Prudish says 'tis very good;
That she's a judge is fully understood."

Gregson asserts, but it is surely a malicious libel, that he picked up from the floor a small scrap of paper on which some ardent admirer of the Waverley Novels had written, " Pray send me any of the Scottish tails."*

Turning now from the past to the present, we may at once say that, like many youthful radicals, the library has settled down into an old age, not untinged with mellow conservative flavour. The number of volumes probably exceeds 25,000, the subscription is a guinea a year, and the shares cost the same sum. For this the members have the use of a magazine-room supplied with the latest forms of periodical pabulum, and the run of a collection which, if not of the first quality, rises a good deal above the ordinary level of circulating libraries. A library that commenced with a donation of Cook's Voyages ought to be well stocked with travellers' tales. This is the case in the present instance. There is an unwise tendency with some to depreciate the value of **old** travels. So far from being mere lumber, they are the storehouse from which the anthropologist must chiefly draw his facts. The old traveller had often the disadvantage of being destitute of scientific spirit, but he at least was free from its bias. What

* [Gregson's] Gimcrackiana. 1833. Pp. 78 to 87.

was seen by an open-eyed observer, determined that
he would "nothing extenuate nor set down aught
in malice," will have more value than the laboured
learning of a pedant. It is only by a careful study
and grouping of the facts told by early explorers
that we can get accurate information as to particular
races or safely generalize on the history of culture.
Of the less known books in this group we may
name M'Kenney's splendid folios relating to the
American Indians, Dr. Hawks's account of the
American expedition to Japan, and nearer home
Landmann's description of Portugal.

Closely allied is the section of archæology. Here
we may name Montfaucon's Antiquité Expliqué,
Layard's Monuments of Nineveh, Meyrick's Ancient
Armour, Cotman's Sepulchral Brasses, and Carter s
architectural works. These are all finely illustrated
folios. Then there is Gwillim's Heraldry for
those who delight in "tricks of arms." The
best edition of the Antiquarian Repertory,
in which matter interesting and valuable is
mixed up inextricably with that which is
simply puerile, should not be passed in silence.
There are many topographical books. Dugdale's
Monasticon and History of St. Paul's, Cave's Antiquities of York, Ackermann's Tour of the Lakes,
Lyson's Magna Britannia, Hoare's South Wilts are all
worth naming, though curiously unequal in point of
importance. Nearer home we find John Whitaker's
visionary History of Manchester, and T. D. Whitaker's
Histories of Richmondshire and Craven, and of
greater importance, the original edition of Ormerod's
History of Cheshire. To this class belongs Surtees'

History of Durham, though apparently without the continuation by Raine. There are several of Pennant's rambling books.

The historical section contains a fair series of modern historians. A work little known in England is Lossing's Field-book of the Revolution, containing pictures with pen and pencil of the localities on which took place the actions giving birth to the American nation. The very valuable Monumenta Historica Britannica has a place on the shelves. With this may be named Palgrave's Parliamentary Writs. We may also bracket together Walker's Sufferings of the Clergy and Neal's History of the Puritans.

A library that for three quarters of a century has had a magazine room ought to be rich in periodicals. There are long sets of many of the reviews and literary journals, including a number that have now ceased to exist. The best writers during the present century have spent no small portion of their strength in this direction. Lovers of Leigh Hunt and Carlyle are well aware that many noble fragments of their work lie buried in these tombs. Taste changes so rapidly from year to year that it is possible very few disturb these old files of the Gentleman's Magazine, the Monthly Chronicle, the Annual Register, the Quarterly and Edinburgh and Retrospective Reviews. Amongst them we noticed a copy of Cruikshank's Omnibus "full inside" of the creatures to which his vigorous imagination has given "a local habitation and a name." There are also other productions of his facile pencil fittingly accompanied by similar volumes from the pencils of Leech, Tenniel, and Doyle. An example of art work in a very different direction is the magnificent volume of nature-printed ferns by Lindley and Moore.

Of the works belonging to literature and literary history there are many that might be named. The student of Celtic genius will be glad to find here Lady Charlotte Guest's Mabinogion, that fine collection of old Welsh legends; he may perhaps even find some help from Walker's Irish Bards. There is a poor copy of Dibdin's Bibliomania, and a fine one of the rare reprint by Joseph Haslewood of Ancient Critical Essays upon English Poets and Poësy. (London. 1811.) Of the privately printed books which Mr. Halliwell has from time to time issued we may cite the Literature of the 16th and 17th Centuries, the Contributions to Early English Literature, Bp. Grosseteste's Castle of Love, and the Yorkshire Anthology. The latter shows that the dialect of the neighbouring county found literary expression at a much earlier date than our own. The publications of several of the printing clubs will be found here, as, for example, the Chetham, Camden, Holbein, and Percy Societies.

The library has now found a home in King-street, where we trust it may long flourish vigorously. It has recently taken stock of its possessions, and issued an Index-Catalogue, compiled by Mr. R. H. Sutton, on the plan introduced by Dr. Crestadoro for the lending departments of the Free Library. The titles are too concise to have much bibliographical value, but the catalogue serves its purpose of supplying a simple and accurate clue to the contents of the library.

Some confusion has occasionally arisen owing to the existence of a previous subscription library in Manchester. At the sale of the Old Subscription Library a number of its books were bought for its younger rival. A notice of this now extinct institution will be found in another part of this volume.

XI.

LANCASHIRE INDEPENDENT COLLEGE.

The Lancashire Independent College was founded in 1842, and may be taken to represent the relations of dissent to modern culture. There have never been wanting learned men amongst the Nonconformists, but it was only natural that their exclusion from the "twin founts" of English learning should have had a bad influence upon the standard of the attainments of the rank and file of their preachers. Some of our greatest scholars have not "been reared in Academic bowers." Some of our finest writers have been equally destitute of scholastic training. Men like Carey and Bunyan however cannot be counted upon *ad libitum*. Nor could a preacher sympathise or grapple with the doubts and difficulties of the present day unless his own mind were also suffused with its many-sided and many-coloured intellectual light. Notwithstanding stereotyped expressions about "vain human learning," it may well be doubted if Dissenters have ever really rated it at a low figure. The Nonconformist academies of the last century certainly did good work.

The Lancashire Independent College originated in private lessons given by the Rev. William Roby to candidates for the ministry. The Independents as an organised body are of recent growth in Lancashire, and earnest young men anxious to become shepherds in Israel had either to go to the Yorkshire institutions

or shift for themselves by private study. Hence the
commencement of Mr Roby's classes. In this good
work he was well backed by Mr. Robert Spear, a
Manchester trader, of whom an American said that,
" while he preferred the English merchants to those
of any other nation, he preferred Mr. Spear to any of
the English merchants."* At the collection after a
missionary sermon he once placed £300 on the plate.
The "class" developed into an academy at Blackburn,
and this on its principal, the Rev. Joseph Fletcher,
leaving for Stepney, was transformed into the
Lancashire Independent College, the first stone of
which was laid in 1840.

The college forms a noble ornament to the pleasant
suburb of Whalley Range. The structure is a fine
one, and with the gardens around it make one think
that the lines of its half hundred of students have
fallen in pleasant places. The long library room has
its windows looking on to lawn and shrubbery.
Turning to the well-lined walls there is much to
interest. The books here indicate pretty clearly the
drift of the work that is being done. Naturally
the theological element preponderates. Could the
dumb souls here bound give vocal expression
to that which is within, what a discordant

---

* Mr. Robert Spear received the two first bags of
American Sea Island Cotton ever imported into England,
and sold them early in 1791 to Robert Owen, afterwards
famous as the apostle of socialism. It was to a sister of
Mr Spear that he owed his first introduction to the
daughter of David Dale, of New Lanark. Whatever
disappointments attended his public career, his domestic
life was one of serene happiness

Babel there would be!   Mutely calm are orthodox
and heterodox.   Calvin, Suarez, Henry More, and
Locke slumber side by side on one shelf.   There are
many fine Biblical works.   Amongst them are two
copies of Walton's Polyglot, one Republican and one
Royalist.   In one copy have been carefully preserved
the original circulars addressed to the patrons of
that great work, which is sometimes said to have
been the first published by subscription.   This,
however, is not correct as Minsheu's Dictionary, 1618,
contains a list of subscribers.   There is also the
Parisian Polyglot in ten volumes.   There are various
printed editions of early biblical codices (Bezae
Augiensis, Claromontanus, and so forth).   There
are various special editions of the Bible worthy to
be described at greater length did space allow, but
we can only name the series of modern versions published by the British and Foreign Bible Society.
The collection of the Fathers and of early writers on
the Church appears to be extensive, nor has the
modern cultus of science prevailed here to the over-
throwing of a long array of classics.   With these
we may place Orelli and Henzen's Latin Inscriptions.
The Apuleius (1501) may also be named, and the
collections of Fabricius.   Returning to ecclesiastical
matters the long set of the Councils by Labbe should
be noticed, and the work by Herman von der Hardt
on the Council of Constance.   The Jena edition of
Luther (1555-58) forms a fine and interesting work.
An interesting companion to it is the folio of his
Table Talk (1729) with its pleasant picture on
the title page of a frugal banquet of th
learned.   Luther sits at the head of the table, and

is conversing with pleasant calmness to a group of his fellow-scholars.

The Puritans are well represented. Prynne's "Treachery of Papists' (1643) and other works testify to the vehemence and learning of

This grand scripturient paper-spiller,
This endless heedless margin-filler,

who was truly a man of an unbounded stomach for all sorts of indigestible learning. Pleasanter to look at are the tomes of Master Perkins, whose "godly" writings were favourites with good Humphrey Chetham. On the other side we have Heylyn's "Life of Laud" (1628) and other works by "lying Peter."

The historical section contains some books of importance, though it is not so strong as the theological department. Thus we have the Monasticon, and Barante's Histoire des Ducs de Bourgogne. For the reverence we owe to the character of Sir Roger de Coverley we are pleased to find here the "Chronicles of Sir Richard Baker." Of special interest for denominational history are the collections respecting the legal contentions over Lady Howley's Charity.

Amongst the miscellaneous works the Encyclopédie and the discursive erudition of Peter Bayle are noticeable. The Classical Museum and Philological Museum contain treasures of critical illustration unfortunately little known. One of the oldest of the reviews is the History of the Works of the Learned, from 1699 to 1710, now rarely met with in anything like a complete state. The modern reviews are well represented, not forgetting, of course, the Eclectic and the British Quarterly.

A smaller room, containing some of the more valuable of the books named, is dedicated to the memory of Dr. Raffles. A glass case contains several volumes of his MS. sermons. There are also some beautiful MSS. presented by Councillor Joseph Thompson, who has been a liberal benefactor. These include several missals of the fourteenth century, one, with a calendar, from Archbishop Tenison's library. Of the same century is a MS. by Nicholas de Lyra. The exquisite workmanship of the monks shows to advantage even by the side of the fine missal printed by Plantin. A part of the Koran written on leaves in Tamil characters carries us back to very primitive literary methods. Beside it are some Egyptian amulets, and an un-opened roll of papyrus also from the land of the Sphinx. Many centuries this Asian mystery has waited for solution. The literature of Egypt is really a voice from the tomb. The monuments show us something of the history and even of the daily life, but it is from the papyri buried with the dead that our scholars have read the poems, the fairy tales, the " wise saws and modern instances " that may have been familiar to the quarrelsome Egyptian whom Moses slew. An interesting object in this case is a silver crucifix, which the label affirms to be " early Christian." The cross was used as a sacred symbol even before the birth of Jesus, but the image of the crucifix was not known until the sixth century, and the present example is later than that period.

There are a number of portraits, not always very flattering. These chiefly represent Puritan divines and their successors. Many of them were connected with this locality. There are Dr. John Owen, Henry Newcome, Thomas Jollie. Timothy Jollie, John Bryan, James Owen, Richard Baxter, Matthew Henry, George Whitfield, Dr. Fletcher, Rev. William Roby, Dr. Wardlaw, Rev. W. L. Alexander, Dr. Vaughan, and Dr. Raffles. There are two unknown divines, supposed to be William Bates and William Bridge. There is a portrait of Mr. Robert Spear, already named, and another of the Rev. James Hervey, M.A., a pious divine, known to the ingenuous youth of half a century ago for his persistent but feeble contemplations of the starry heavens.

XII.

THE FRIENDS.

Is it in compensation for their gift of vocal silence that the Quakers have been endowed with the vast scripturiency which has marked them as a sect? They sprang into being in Cromwell's day, and yet by 1719 they had published over four thousand books and tracts. They printed substantial editions, and had their books translated into various tongues. Their mission, they held, was one for all mankind, and they would not put their light under a bushel. They printed letters to the Great Turk and to the greater Protector of England, to the Emperor of China, and to all manner of people high and low, and wrought with an intensity of missionary zeal that defied the personal outrage, fines, and imprisonment to which they were subjected. They not only made history but they wrote it. The history of English Dissent has few pages sublimer than those recording the early history of the religious Society of Friends. They were the scorn alike of the Churchman and the Nonconformist. They lived up to their religion, and it brought them into antagonism with the ruling powers at every point. When the King wanted men, they would not fight; when the magistrate wanted a witness, they would not swear; when the squire wanted them to be "respectful" they declined to doff their hats; when the parson wanted money, they refused to pay tithes. They denounced the Nonconformist minister as a diviner for hire, equally with his clerical brethren. Persecution utterly failed to tame them.

With all this fierce enthusiasm they were so gentle
and inoffensive, so honest in their dealings, so clean
in their life, that their very jailers loved them and
were sometimes more merciful than the law.   In a
later age, when the law had finally abandoned the
hope of bending them to the pattern of the Established Church, they turned their enthusiasm to the
service of humanity, and were earnest helpers of
movements intended to lessen suffering and
crime.   Of their latest developments we need
not speak, nor speculate whether they are
doomed to extinction, or simply wait for some
coming "furnace-blast" that shall bring with it the
glories as well as " the pangs of transformation."

The Meeting-House at Manchester, said to be the
largest in the kingdom, contains two distinct libraries.
The most valuable is that known as the Midgley
Reference Library.   It consists of 146 volumes,
relating to the early history of the Quakers.   There
are fifty-six volumes of tracts, many of them containing over two dozen pamphlets.   The collection
was formed by Mr. J. Midgley, of Rochdale, and
must have cost a good deal, both of time and money,
to bring together.   He has noted on a copy of
George Bishope's "Cry of Blood" that it cost him
18s., and was the " dearest tract" he ever got.   His
children presented it to the Lancashire and Cheshire
Quarterly Meeting.   A carefully compiled catalogue
has been printed :—

Midgley Reference Library: Catalogue of Books relating to the Society of Friends, the gift of the surviving
children of the late James Midgley, of Spring Hill,
Rochdale, to Lancashire and Cheshire Quarterly Meeting,
9th month 17th, 1863.   Manchester, 1866, 12mo.

The Midgley collection contains many of the books issued by Fox, Dewsbury, Margaret Fell, and other early Quakers. There is a volume of scarce pamphlets written by Isaac Pennington before he joined the despised sect. A sect which springs to birth during a time of high-wrought religious feeling, which has a leaven of the mystical in it, and which is subjected to bitter reviling and persecution, is certain to develop something of a prophetical literature. So we find in 1660 a "strange prophecy presented to the King's Most Excellent Majesty by a woman Quaker all in white, called Ahivah," who claims to have foretold his coming to the throne, and entreats from him "toleration for the saints." To the same year belongs the vision of Humphrey Smith in May, 1660, in which Frost Fair and the Fire of London are foretold.

At first one might wonder to find here the old Arabic romance of Hai Ebn Yokdhan. It is, however, easily explained, and arises from a reference to it in the Apology of Barclay, who cites it in illustration of the doctrine of the sufficiency of the inner light. It was written by Abu Jaafar Ebn-Tophail in the twelfth century, and is a philosophical romance of considerable interest and ingenuity. There are two English translations, the best being that by Ockley, made directly from the original. It is the story of a baby cast on an uninhabited island. Suckled by a roe, Hai manages to grow up strong and healthy, invents for himself many of the arts, and shows how, as the author believes, "one may by the mere light of nature attain the knowledge of things natural and supernatural ; more particularly the knowledge of

God and the affairs of another life." This notion of
the education of nature has had an attraction for
many minds. Rousseau proposed to confine Emilius
to the reading of Robinson Crusoe on some such
ground, but as Campe observes, Robinson is by no
means so badly off as he might be, as he saves some
tools and seeds from the wreck of the ship. A distinguished living scholar began to translate Robinson
Crusoe into Latin, but found this objection so
strong that he modified the text until it assumed the
aspect of an independent work, having a philosophical interest of its own as showing the possible
exegesis of human arts. This work still remains
unpublished. Campe's Robinson der Jungere has
perhaps more philosophy, but it has certainly less
talent then its prototype.

The early Friends were exceedingly plain-spoken
in their book titles, which were often very long and
very uncomplimentary to the other side. Thus John
Bolton replies to Nathaniel Smith, "a shoemaker,
who, being ashamed of his own trade, styles himself
in his book student of physic." "Cain's bloody
race known by their fruits" is the title of one
Howgill's exercises, whilst Fox sends a message
"to all the people who meet in steeple houses in
England." One of these tracts recalls to memory
the honourable part the Friends have taken against
slavery. It needed more courage than the bulk of
mankind possess for Benjamin Lay to assert in
Philadelphia in the year 1737 that "all slave
keepers that keep the innocent in bondage" were
apostates to the Christian faith.

The Friends have never limited their belief in
inspiration to one sex, nor do they think it part of

the "whole duty of woman" to subdue and repress whatever genius may have been given. Here are the "Fruits of Retirement," of Mary Mollineux of Liverpool, who could fluently discourse in Latin and, with some knowledge of Greek, was also skilful in the preparation of simples, "had a good understanding of physick and chyrurgery," and a love of poetry, if she lacked the power of expression. This kind-hearted creature, who delighted in using her knowledge for the benefit of the poor, met her future husband in Lancaster Castle, where they were both prisoners for attending a religious meeting. Mary Mollineux was "not free" to print her poems during her life-time, but her admiring husband issued them after her death in 1695. In 1690 she had some discourse with "Dr. Stratford (so called), Bishop of the Diocess of Cheshire and Lancashire." The lady claimed to have the best of the argument; the Bishop was unwilling to persecute, and begged his officer if possible to let them have their liberty, "and do what kindness you can for them."

Enthusiasm and pedantry kiss together amongst the early Friends. They had the martyr-spirit. They would have died at the stake with cheerful composure rather than deny the doctrine of the inner light, or put off the hat to a magistrate. It was equally heretical in their eyes to acknowledge the Pope, or to scrape backwards the foot. Their vehemence was aroused equally at the ungodly and the ungrammatical usages of the age. In the same year in which George Fox addressed a communication "to all the nations under the whole heavens" concerning his religious views, he also sent forth a "Battle-door for teachers and professors to

learn singular and plural, you to many thou to one."
The book is divided into parts, each having a title-
page in the figure of a battle-dore, with a motto and
the initials of George Fox. The languages given
are "English, Latine, Italian, Greek, Hebrew, Caldee,
Syriack, Arabick, Persiack, Ethiopick, Samaritan,
Coptick or Egyptick, Armenian, Saxon, Welsh,
Mence, Cornish, French, Spanish, Portugal, High-
Dutch, Low-Dutch, Danish, Bohemian, Slavonian ;"
and there are also "some examples in the Polo-
nian, Lithuanian, Irish, and East Indian; together
with the singular and plural words, ' thou '
and ' you,' in Swedish, Turkish, Muscovian, and
Curlandian tongues." This book was compiled by
John Stubbs and Benjamin Furley, with some additions by Fox, who was then in durance in Lancaster
Castle. As he was ignorant of every language but
his own, and not very immaculate in his orthography
even of that, it is pretty certain that Fox could not
have had much concern in it. The frequent occurrence of his initials in it is sarcastically commented
upon by Francis Bugg, who, from an enthusiastic
follower, became a bitter opponent.

Here is one of their early tracts, with a certain
pathos about its dingy leaves. It is a petition to the
Parliament of England, an appeal from the Quaker
women against the enforcement of tithes. This
dead question was hot and hard enough in 1659.
Seven thousand signed their names to this prayer.
Ah, poor Dorcas and Ruth, vainly hoping that
God would put it into the hearts of the rulers
to send them back husband and lover who were
festering in the prison-house! It strikes one as

oddly appropriate that this paper should be "printed for Mary Westwood."

There is very much more of interest about the Midgley books, were there space to enter more fully into their contents. The other library belongs to "Manchester Meeting," and has a catalogue. It is, however, a mere list, not always very explicit. Thus, a volume which the catalogue styles "Ancient Tracts" contains several papers by William Dewsbury and others, and at the end a contemporary pamphlet relating to that black episode in New England history, the martyrdom of Mary Dyer. The title-page succinctly states the case of the Quakers: "A Declaration of the sad and great persecution and martyrdom of the people of God called Quakers in New-England for the worshipping of God. Whereof 22 have been banished upon pain of death, 03 have been MARTYRED. 03 have had their Right-Ears cut. 01 have been burned in the hand with the letter H. 31 Persons have received 650 Stripes. 01 was beaten while his Body was like a jelly. Several were beat with Pitched Ropes. Five Appeals made to England were denied by the Rulers of Boston. One thousand forty-four pounds worth of goods hath been taken from them (being poor men) for meeting together in the fear of the Lord, and for keeping the commands of Christ. One now lyeth in fetters, condemned to dye." The Puritans who had left England to enjoy liberty of conscience determined that no Quaker should be tolerated in Boston. The penalty of disobedience to this law of banishment was death, and this penalty was inflicted upon William Robinson, Marmaduke

Stephenson, and Mary Dyer. She was "of a comely and grave countenance" and well stricken in years.

The library consists almost exclusively of Friends' books. A copy of the Bible of 1540 may, however, be named. There is a richness and variety about the biographical literature, especially of the Quakers, that ought to be better known. What can be finer than the story of Thomas Lurting? From being a fighting sailor under our sea king, Blake, he became "a harmless Christian." After this he was on board a ship that was captured by an Algerine pirate. Lurting's influence with the English seamen was so great that they followed his instructions, and, without spilling blood, turned the tables upon their captors. The Turks, instead of being sold as slaves, were put ashore near Algiers. Of the better known Friends we need not speak. There is a long roll of them who "loved their fellow-men," and of whom their works do testify.

XIII.

THE CORPORATION LIBRARY AT THE TOWN HALL.

There are probably a good many citizens of Manchester who are not aware that before the foundation of the Free Libraries the Town Council had already established a public library. Attenders of meetings which are held from time to time in the Mayor's Parlour will probably have noticed a number of tall volumes clad in Quaker garb. These sober tomes form no inconsiderable portion of the library of the Corporation of Manchester, the remainder being shelved in the ante-room. The library may be said to have commenced in August, 1844, when the late Mark Philips, M.P., presented a set of Hansard's Parliamentary Debates, "to be deposited in the Town Hall for reference by the inhabitants of the borough, under such regulations as the Town Council may think proper." The donation was made, however, with the knowledge that a collection of books was in contemplation. The views of the promoters were expressed in a memorandum, also read at the August meeting of the Town Council:—

The advantage of possessing, for the use of the Council of the borough, a library containing the best constitutional, legal, historical, and statistical works of our country and period, will be readily admitted, even by those who may be inclined to doubt the necessity of making such a collection at the public expense. With a view to convince all parties of the advantages to be derived from the opportunity of ready and constant reference to works of the above character, the undersigned have presented to the Corporation the works which are hereinafter named, and which they hope may form a nucleus of a library which will be found most useful to the members for the time-being of the Town Council, and will hereafter become worthy of the community of which they are the representatives In this hope, and with this view, they have been joined by our excellent representative, Mark Philips, Esq, whose munificent present has this day been communicated to the council. Upon the application of the Mayor, supported by Mr Philips, Sir James Graham, as Secretary of State for the Home Department, has presented, as already reported, a copy of the Public Records to the Corporation.   ALEXANDER KAY, Mayor.

THOMAS POTTER.

WILLIAM NIELD

JAMES KERSHAW.

The books presented at this date included the journals of the Houses of Parliament, the statutes at large, and other books on law and statistics. The other donors were Mr. Kay, Sir Thomas Potter, Alderman Kershaw, and Alderman William Nield. Mr. Philips afterwards gave about 500 volumes of parliamentary reports from 1833 to 1840. At the commencement £100 was spent on the library, and in September 1845 it was resolved to appropriate a sum not exceeding £50 annually for its maintenance and increase.

In 1846 Mr. Alexander Kay being in Paris, inspecting the markets and abattoirs, received for the library five volumes relating to the municipal affairs of the French capital, from the Prefect of the Seine, the Comte de Rambuteau. Various donations were received from persons nearer home.

Thus, the Literary and Philosophical Society contributed a set of its Memoirs. Mr. F. R. Atkinson urged upon the founders the importance of collecting books illustrative of local history. An interesting contribution in this direction was presented by Mr. Lowndes, of Liverpool, who sent a volume of tracts formerly belonging to the Rev. Joshua Brookes, the eccentric chaplain of the Old Church. These pamphlets described, in prose and verse, the Manchester of a century ago. The volume is described at length by the late Mr. Harland, in his Manchester Collectanea, to which the reader is referred for fuller particulars. The local books are comparatively few, but there are the Foundations of Manchester, King's Vale Royal, and some others.

The long set of the Causes Célèbres should perhaps be classed with the law books. There is a grim interest attaching to these records of crime and wrong-doing. In reading some it seems pretty certain that the greatest criminals in the court were not in the dock. The longer array of Howell's State Trials is a still more important book. In it we have not only details of human wickedness that almost defy belief, but of the sufferings of those by whom our English liberties were won.

The particulars already given will show to some extent the character of the library. It contains several county histories of value, such as Blomefield's Norfolk and Hutchinson's Durham. To this topographical class belong Grose's Antiquities. Of more general interest are the Somers Tracts and Harleian Miscellany, vast repertories of the wisdom and unwisdom of our ancestors. Much matter relating to early history and law is concealed in the publication of the old Record Commission. These volumes were presented by Sir James Graham in 1843. They illustrate almost every phase of our past national life. Scarcely one of them can be dipped into without some quaint revelation of the good old times. What a light is thrown upon the spirit of the age in which John Lackland lived by the entries in his roll of expenses. Thus 9s. 4½d. was given to one hundred paupers whom the King feasted at Lambeth, because he had eaten flesh twice on Friday. At Northampton a thousand paupers were entertained, 500 being fed with bread, flesh, and ale, and 500 with bread, fish, and ale. When the King had successful sport, he seems to have made a point of feasting some poor folk. William, the man of Adam Crok, received a shilling each for six Welshmen's heads which he brought to the King at Rochester.

The publications of the old Record Commission are not supplemented by the more recent series issued under the authority of the Master of the Rolls. We should be entering upon a large field in attempting to speak of the deficiencies of the collection. It is really in a state of arrested development. Very little has been done towards increasing it since the first few years of its existence. An exception, must be made in relation to parliamentary papers which appear to have been added regularly year by year. Reference has been made in the course of these articles to the valuable matter to be found in the papers printed by order of Parliament. They form a huge storehouse of important facts relating to the social, commercial, and sanitary aspects of modern life. Of their interest from a scientific and archæological point of view we need not now speak. This is undoubtedly the most important part of the collection. The Corporation Library is still, however, after thirty years of existence the barest rudiment of what a municipal library should be. The ideal set forth by its founders has not been fulfilled. A collection of books intended primarily for the use of the Town Council and its officials, and in a secondary degree as a reference library for the citizens, need not be very large, but would certainly have to be far more extensive than the present one. It should contain a good number of books of reference, strictly so called, both English and foreign, ranging from the British Almanac to Ersch and Grüber's great Encyclopædia. It should contain also the more important statistical works relating to British possessions and to foreign states. Special care should be given to the collection of books which illustrate the history of municipal bodies at home and abroad, and show the gradual development of local self-government. The documents which trace the evolution of the modern town councils from the old guilds should be accessible to those who are asked to give the name of Guildhall to the municipal palace of a city that never had a secular guild at all. Another class of books important for a municipal library are those works published by some of the continental and American cities. A good type of this class is the statistical account of Prague compiled by Professor Joseph Erben, which gives an almost microscopic view of all relating to that city. In addition to this, there should be works explanatory of the legal and constitutional conditions of our country. A collection built up on the lines thus indicated could not fail to be of value to all who are interested—and who is not?—in the manner in which our municipal work is done.

There is a MS. catalogue of the library compiled by Mr. Edward Edwards. Some of the books appear to have been misplaced, and on our last visit a few of the volumes named were not accessible.

XIV.

HOLY TRINITY CHURCH, SALFORD.

In the " good old times," when there was not so distinctly visible as now the line of demarcation between things sacred and things secular, the Church was to a large extent the centre of social as well as of religious life. Thus we find the play of Robin Hood and Maid Marian was acted within the Parish Church of Manchester, in Queen Mary's reign. If the ancient churchyards served for fair grounds, and the churches themselves for occasional theatres, we need not be surprised to find that some portions of the building should at times have been appropriated for libraries. There is one at Langley Marsh, of which Charles Knight has left a charming description. Its dusty folios have an added interest because John Milton's hand may have turned over their leaves of ancient eloquence and erudition. Our own district is not without a few collections of this class. Humphrey Chetham left money for the purchase of books to be placed in the churches of Manchester, Bolton, Walmsley, Turton, and Gorton. With the exception of those at the two last places, the books have now disappeared. A less known collection is that still preserved at the Holy Trinity Church, Salford.

The founder of the church was a worthy merchant of Manchester, whose portrait would form a fitting companion to that of Humphrey Chetham, as drawn by Fuller. It has been finely sketched by Hollingworth. Of Humphrey Booth he says: " Hee was a man just in his trading, generous in entertainment of any gentlemen of quality that came to the towne though meere strangers to him, bountifull to the church and poore, faithful to his friend, and we hope God gave him both repentance for and remission of his sinns in the blood of Jesus." The building and endowing of the church was done at the cost of Humphrey Booth, with the exception of £200 subscribed by a number of persons, of whom Sir Alexander Radcliffe, of Ordsal, was the first. It is an interesting trait in the character of Booth, the founder, that " being by God's blessing on his trading made rich," he gave to the poor of Salford " the first lands that he bought to the value of twenty pounds per annum and paid it duely all his lifetime." His earnest desire that he might see the chapel built and partake of the communion in it was gratified, but the weakness which had threatened his life was only conquered by the strength of this craving, and when it had been satisfied " he was never able to goe forth after, nor scarce to get home." This was in 1634. The donor of the library was a descendant of the founder of the church. Humphrey Booth, the founder, married Elizabeth, daughter of Robert Whitworth of Newton, by whom he had two sons, (1) Robert, who married a daughter of Oswald Mosley; (2) Humphrey (Humphrey Booth of Blackley), who by his wife Ann had issue two daughters and a son Humphrey (Humphrey Booth the younger), who was a benefactor of the Church and of Salford. One of the daughters, Sarah, married James Davenport; the other married John Oldfield, a woollen draper. They had two sons. The first was named after his father. The second, Humphrey Oldfield, was born in December 27, 1657, and was buried in the Collegiate Church at Manchester, November 25, 1690. It was he who presented the books to the church.

The library was in the tower of the church, but the danger from damp led to their removal to the vestry where they still remain, filling a small old-fashioned book-case. The books are a mere handful, not more than sixty or seventy volumes, but the tradition is that at the period early in the present century, when they were put in order, a number were rejected and cast out as waste paper. It is quite possible that from a bibliographical point of view these would have greater interest than those which were retained. There are here in impressive folios several of the fathers of the English Church. Many persons who do not endorse all their views will, like " Jonas Fisher," confess to an appreciative regard for the sober eloquence of these divines of " the good old-fashioned stately school."

> So full o' manly simple faith,
> So rich in warmth and sweet content;
> No harsh malignant threatenings,
> No cold hard-hearted arguments.

The writings of Hammond, Reynolds, Tillotson, Bramhall, Sanderson, Tenison, and Jeremy Taylor, represent the staple of the library. There are also some minor works of a controversial character. The only book of immediate local interest seems to be a copy of the Dissuasive from Revenge, written by Dr. Nicholas Stratford, once Warden of the Collegiate Church, and afterwards Bishop of Chester. This book is dedicated to the inhabitants of Manchester and Salford.

Taking down a volume of Bishop Hall we are confronted with the portrait (by Crispin van Quebarren) of that eminent divine, followed by these lines :—

> How farre beyond a Picture is his worth,
> Whome Pen, nor Pencill, truly can set forth !
> Behold his Reuerend FACE, his better PART,
> As left ungravd this was beyond all Art.
>
> His Holy Thoughts in sacred MEDITATIONS,
> His ravisht SOULE in the heavenly CONTEMPLATIONS
> Could not bee drawne. Heere only are his Lookes—
> The Pictures of the rest are in his Bookes.
>
> I. SAMPSON.

Sampson can hardly be said to be a strong man in the "golden land of poesy." The number of verses on the inadequate powers of portraiture has been well commented upon by Mr. F. Hendricks in the pleasant pages of *Notes and Queries* (5th s. iv. 363). Sampson's conceit has been applied alike to Shakspere and to Salmon the empiric.

The collection includes a fine copy of the edition of Foxe's Book of Martyrs, issued in 1631. This, like the first edition, is illustrated with woodcuts, vigorous both in drawing and engraving. The credit of Foxe's book has been rudely shaken since the days when, in company with the great Bible, it was chained to reading-desks in the churches as a great fountain of Protestant ardour and earnestness. There is also a volume of the Mirror of Saints and Sinners (1671), written by Samuel Clarke, who roundly accused Dr. Thomas Fuller of plagiarizing

from his stores. Fuller replied that he had perused
Clarke's lucubrations "as travellers by the Levitical
Law were permitted to pass through men's vine-
yards. For they must eat their fill on condition,
they put no grapes up in their vessel." He denied the
accusation, "detesting such felony," and was certainly
not likely to steal from Clarke, whom a caustic critic
of the time termed "a severe Calvinist and a
scribbling plagiary."

We need only add that the books given by
Humphrey Oldfield appear to have been the divinity-
books bought for his own use. He also bequeathed
£20 for their increase. Some of the volumes have been
annotated by the Rev. William Verdon, formerly
rector of the church. The benevolent intentions of
Humphrey Oldfield have not been crowned with the
success he desired. The books are not lent out, nor
are they at all read in their present position. They
would have more chance of being used and useful if
they formed part of some public library. The donor
certainly did not desire them to remain unread from
generation to generation. Is not an arrangement
which would, by gift, loan, or purchase, place them
in the Chetham Library, or in the Salford Free
Library, worth the consideration of all concerned?

THE CATHEDRAL.

The first public library for the people of Manchester was connected with the Old Church. Its situation was in the Jesus Chapel or chantry founded by the munificence of Roger Bexwyke the younger, at the beginning of the sixteenth century. The priests of the chantry were by deed placed upon a footing of equality with the fellows of the college, in recognition of the liberal gifts which Bexwyke had made towards the adornment and enhancement of the church. When the chantries were dissolved Robert Prestwicke, priest of "Byssykes" chantry, had a pension of £4. 1s. 9d. On the accession of Elizabeth the Jesus Chapel appears to have passed into the possession of Isabel Beck, widow of Richard Bexwick. She sold it for twenty nobles to Francis Pendleton and Cecily his wife, who were her daughter and son-in-law. The younger son and ultimately heir of this couple, was Henry Pendleton, who, in 1653, "sold it or gave it, (being very ruinous, and the roof fallen down, and the lead sold or stolen) to the town of Manchester to be an English library." The necessity for such an appropriation of the chapel had arisen from the liberality of another benefactor of the town. This was John Prestwych, B.D., and a fellow of All Souls' College, Oxford. He gave "several books unto the inhabitants of the town of Manchester to be kept within some convenient place within the

said town for a library for the use of the said town."
Such is the phrase in which Henry Pendleton, Edward Johnson, and James Lancashire by deed conveyed the chantry to sixteen gentlemen of the neighbourhood in trust as a library room. These trustees were bound to pay to Pendleton, Johnson, and Lancashire, "the yearly rent of one penny" at each Christmas, if demanded.

What became of Prestwych's gift would now be a vain question to ask. So far as we know, not even a list of the books has ever been discovered. The money paid for burials in the chapel was, according to one statement, to be applied to the maintenance of this library. One of the trustees, nominated in 1653, was Humphrey Chetham, the founder, whose will, already made, contained not only provision for the foundation of the noble library which now bears his name, but also a bequest of £200 to be bestowed "in Godly English books, such as Calvin's, Preston's and Perkins' works . . to be . . chained upon desks, or to be fixed to the pillars, or in other convenient places in the parish churches of Manchester and Boulton-in-the-Moors, and in the chapels of Turton, Walmsley, and Gorton." Chetham died in 1653, and after some delay the Manchester share of "Godly books" bought by his bequest were placed in the Jesus Chapel. The task was performed by Henry Newcome, whose diary contains various references to the English Library, as the bequest of Prestwych and Chetham appears to have been styled. The books remained in the church until somewhere about 1830, when they were either sold by the churchwardens or removed to the Chetham Library and sold by the authorities of that institution. At the time of their dispersal they are said to have numbered about a hundred volumes in bad condition from use and neglect. Some of them with the chains still attached were bought by the president of the Chetham Society in an old bookshop in this city.

One would like to think that the warden, fellows, clerks, and choristers who formed the "Guild of the Blessed Virgin in Manchester," and who performed the services of the Collegiate Church were not unmindful of literature. Some books they must have possessed, if only those from which they might read perchance

> The legend of good St. Guthlac
> And St. Basil's homilies.

Archbishop Langley's will, dated in 1436, contains a bequest to the College of Mamcestre of a book called "Flores Bernardi." This would not improbably be a selection from the works ot the great mediæval theologian St. Bernard of Clairvaux. One of the fellows of the college made himself a pleasant retreat near "the High Knolls," where he enclosed a pool with hedges and seats. This place constructed, as Hollingworth surmises, "possibly for his meditation," was long afterwards known as Sir John Browne's pit. No great stretch of imagination would be needed to suppose that some of his materials for thinking were furnished by the books belonging to the guild. The *Flores Bernardi* and all the other flowers of literature that may have belonged to the Church guild have long since withered or been plucked by felonious hands.

The Cathedral Library which now exists is a

creation of the last few years. The visitor who thinks of the chapter libraries of Lincoln or of Chichester will feel like one sent to spy out not the fulness but the poverty of the land. The books it possesses are good, and do credit to the liberality of their donors; but the collection is quite inadequate for its intended purpose. The number of volumes is about 450. The library is designed for the use of the clergy of the Cathedral, and is strictly one of consultation, no books being permitted out of the room in which the books are kept. That there are any books at all is due to the generosity of Canons Gibson, Richson, and Marsden, and of Dr. Crompton, who have presented very nearly every volume. The first thing that strikes one is the entire absence of patristic literature. The fathers of the Church are represented by the Ante-Nicene Library. With every respect for that useful publication we should be glad to see it supplemented, if not superseded by the Benedictine Editions. The apparatus for the study of the biblical text is equally meagre, Alford's Greek Testament being the most noteworthy part of it. Poole's Synopsis may be named, and also a fine copy of the edition of Philo Judæus, printed at Frankfort in 1691. Passing by Spelman's Concilia, the stream of ecclesiastical history is marked in a sparing manner by such works as Soame's Anglo-Saxon Church, the volumes of Strype, and Selden's History of Tithes (1618), now a rare book. Luther is absent, but the spirit of the Reformation is indicated by the English translation of Calvin, by the manifold publications of the Parker Society, and by the modern edition of Fox's Book of Martyrs. We should not omit to name here a fine folio of the works of the learned Joseph Mede.

The miscellaneous section include Rapin, Froissart and a few other historical books. A fine copy of Grose's Antiquities, and another of the Foundations of Manchester, may be named. Very few volumes have special local interest. There is, however, "An Epistle to a Friend," consisting of verses suggested by a sermon preached by· the Rev. B. Nichols, in which he disputed the "false claims to martyrdom" of the unhappy Manchester men who were executed for their part in the rebellion of 1745. There is a copy of the sermons of Dr. Samuel Ogden, printed at Cambridge in 1780. He was a man of unusual learning, but rude and clownish in appearance. On the accession of George III. he composed three copies of verses, Latin, English, and Arabic. This led to the following epigram, which will bear another repetition :—

> When Ogden, his prosaic verse
>   In Latin numbers drest,
> The Roman language proved too weak
>   To stand the critic's test.
>
> In English rhyme he next essayed
>   To show he'd some pretence,
> But ah! rhyme only would not do,
>   They still expected sense.
>
> Enraged the Doctor swore he'd place
>   On critics no reliance,
> So wrapt his thoughts in Arabic,
>   And bade them all defiance.

The books by Pierius (1678) and Caussin (1631) on hieroglyphics have no practical value, though they are both in a measure curious. The *Zeitgeist* is represented by the Encyclopædia Britannica and sundry volumes of the Social Science Association. Marked by the spirit of another age is a fine Prayer Book, printed in 1706, adorned with silver clasps and containing the office of healing for scrofula. Our English monarchs from Edward the Confessor to Queen Anne are said to have had the power of curing "King's-evil" by their royal touch. Dr. Johnson was touched by that royal lady when he was a child, thirty months old, but with no success. The Jacobites contend that William and Mary and Anne did not possess this "faculty divine." Their monarchical power had in it the vitiating element of popular consent, and was not based entirely upon the hereditary "divine right of kings to govern wrong." The office for healing disappeared from the liturgy about 1719. The Kings of the House of Brunswick do not seem to have tried the experiment. The enemies of the Hanoverians asserted that this princely power remained with the exiled Stuarts. The Old Pretender was said to have cured a man at Avignon, and when the Young Pretender was holding court at Holyrood House, a female child touched by him was asserted to have been cured within three weeks. As the last of the royal Stuarts lies buried at Rome, the only hope of those now so afflicted must be in medical science.

To return from this digression. The small nucleus of a library we have described is evidently tenderly cared for. We hope that by liberal benefactions it may grow into a collection of which its possessors may be justly proud.

XVI. AND XVII.

THE FREE REFERENCE LIBRARY.

The Free Reference Library is the largest public library in the district. It is also the best. It cannot boast of priceless MSS. such as glorify the Chetham Library, nor is it so rich as that collection in the domain of theology and of the general literature of the sixteenth century. Libraries like that of the Medical Society surpass it in special departments, but the fact remains that to students it offers the best general collection in the North of England. There are of course many gaps which need still to be filled up, but considering that the library is not yet a quarter of a century old, and that the extension of the lending libraries has necessarily absorbed a large amount of the public money applicable to library purposes, the result is one which the city may regard with some complacence, and which certainly speaks well for the management of the institution.

The Manchester Free Library system dates from 1852. The Reference Department opened with 16,000 volumes ; it has now about 55,000 volumes. Its weakest parts are probably those of law and medicine, both of which are very inadequately represented. Its strongest departments are those of English History and literature. Its most characteristic feature is its remarkable collection of pamphlet literature, and especially of tracts relating to politics and trade. Even in those sections where its wants are greatest it offers some things worthy of notice.

The works relating to theology and morals are numerically fewer than in any other class. They have, however, been selected in a comprehensive spirit which makes them fairly representative, not only of the broad divisions of the various schools of Christian thought, but also of many of the minuter differences now existing. The long array of editions of the Bible is of interest alike to the theologian and the philologist. The Polyglot of Walton, the *Codex Alexandrinus*, and the editions issued during the sixteenth and seventeenth centuries, form a valuable textual apparatus. The *Codex Siniaticus* is here only in an English edition, but the lover of curiosities may console himself with the presence of the *Codex Mayerianus*—a literary forgery of the nineteenth century. The translations of the Bible include many rare and valuable books. We may name, for instance, the Jews' Bible of Ferrara, the heretical version made by Dr. Geddes, and the edition of the English Testament, printed about 1539. The yellow leaves and quaint woodcuts of the lastnamed forcibly call to mind a period when the Bible had to be printed in secrecy and smuggled into England under pains and penalties. Time brings about strange revenges. Our nation which, three hundred years ago, had no home-printed Bibles, is now the great manufactory from which by missionary zeal they are scattered over the face of the earth. Of the work which is done by the Bible Society the library possesses an interesting memorial in a series of translations of the Bible, or of portions of it, in about 140 langnages. Some of these are spoken by races entirely destitute of literature or of written characters. The missionaries have not only had to learn the language but to adapt the Roman alphabet to its representation, and also to impress upon the wondering savage the connection between the written word and the spoken thought. The Micmac version is printed in Pitman's phonotypy.

Passing from the Bible to its interpretations, and the systems which have been deduced from it, we find most of the sects represented, but in varying degree. One reason for this is that they vary greatly either in the power of literary expression or in the desire to exert it. The followers of Swedenborg have printed an enormous mass of books written by or relating to the Swedish seer, and with rare liberality have presented them freely to many libraries. They have a special relevance here in connection with the important part which Manchester took in the early history of that denomination. The Quakers have in the same way presented many of their best books of exposition and biography. Even the Shakers from their far-off New England settlement sent to the birthplace of their prophetess and founder a copy of their "Testimony" respecting the second appearance of Christ. The Fathers are but scantily represented in original editions, but there are serviceable translations of the most important of them. The same remark applies with some modification to the important theological literature of Modern Germany. A few of these are present in the bad type and worse paper which the Teutons are, thank Heaven, now gradually abandoning, and of the others, at least of the more orthodox section, there are the useful versions issued by the Messrs. Clark, of Edinburgh. The reformers are represented by the Parker Society, and a few original editions. The pillars of the English Church and the great lights of English Dissent are nearly all present.

Nor does the Library include only Christian theology. The creed outworn of Greece and Rome must of course be sought in the classical writers, who are best counted in another department. There are a few Hebrew books, amongst them the Talmud, but the edition is a poor one, from which the passages directed against Christianity have been carefully expunged. There is the sacred book of the Zoroastrian religion, as edited by Pietraszewski, who gave up his life to the task. There are works illustrating various phases of Mahometanism. There is the valuable edition of the Chinese classics edited by Dr. Legge, and forming a cyclopædia of the moral and religious as well as the historical and general literature of the Middle Kingdom. There are works illustrating the doctrines of the Taouist sect, founded by Lau-tze, whose often elevated morality has not prevented his followers from sinking into gross superstition. There are numerous works relating to Buddhism, that mysterious faith which numbers even more adherents than Christianity. Nor have the mythological speculations of other races been ignored. The Scandinavian Eddas and the legends of the Zulus have equally a place. Whoever chooses to engage in the investigation suggested by the newly-created science of religion will not lack for material upon which to operate.

Leaving theology, we enter upon the broad domain of history. The English section is exceedingly well filled and will enable a patient investigator to have a full appreciation of the varied forces which have been at work in these islands since the day when "wild in wood the noble savage ran," down to the present era of civilization. The student so inclined may catch glimpses in the classic writers of our remote ancestors, whose love for mankind sometimes took a cannibalistic turn. In Gildas he may read the groans of the oppressed Britons. Under the imaginative guidance of Geoffroy of Monmouth, he may listen to the fabulous narrative of the colonizing of Britain by Brutus and his Trojan followers. It is to these vain imaginings we owe the grandeur of Shakspere's Lear. He may delight himself with the mediæval chroniclers, full of value for the witness they bear to the spirit of the age even when most unreliable as to facts. Thus Roger of Wendover tells us that where St. John of Beverley lies buried the fiercest bulls become as gentle as so many lambs. Statements like this may be received with the amount of attention that is due to them, without impairing the value of testimony to that which the writers had seen and heard themselves. The chronicles of Froissart, Monstrelet, Fabyan, Grafton, Hall, Holinshed, and others, will carry him down to a period when the modern historical spirit begins to reign. The works of these moderns, of Macaulay, Lingard, Hume, Sharon, Turner, Lappenberg, Froude, and in fact all the prominent writers on English history will enable him to contrast the treatment of events, to compare, select, reject, and gradually form an independent judgment for himself upon any point of our history. If he wishes to go deeper into details there are ample materials in the publications of the old Record Commission, in the learned medleys issued by Tom Hearne, and in the (literally) thousands and thousands of pamphlets dealing with past episodes in the nation's existence, sometimes dimly groping after principles now happily acknowledged, at other times anticipating with eagle glance that which should not be "understanded of the common people" for further generations. The collection of pamphlets and small books relating to past periods of the national life is one that can probably not be matched out of London and Oxford. Amongst the byways of English history we may refer to the extremely interesting collection relating to the so-called "Popish Plot." The extent of this series is remarkable. It contains most of the original publications relating to that nefarious attempt of Oates and Bedloe and their fellow-wretches to swear away the lives of innocent men and bring them to the scaffold for the sake of blood-money. There is also a long series of the tracts of William Prynne and many illustrating the early history of the trades and industries of the country. This is a part of our annals which has been sadly neglected, and yet, as Mr. Smiles has shown, it has often the interest of romance added to the usefulness of truth. The history of textile manufactures, of the rise of the factory system, and the evils by which its earlier stages were marked and the vigorous discussions which preceded their amendment, are to be found in these pamphlets. They contain also remarkable evidence regarding the course of events which in this country have gradually freed the workman from the injurious restrictions to which his forefathers were subjected.

Another storehouse for the illustration of our history is the *London Gazette*. It is doubtful whether a copy so perfect as that possessed by the Manchester Free Reference Library exists elsewhere. Neither the British Museum nor the Bodleian at Oxford can claim that distinction. From its first issue in 1665 to the present day it has been the official depositary of government proclamations, state papers, and so forth. In this connection we may name also the lengthy publications of Hansard and his predecessors, in which are preserved the parliamentary eloquence of our own and past ages. The long sets of the *Gentleman's Magazine*, dating from 1734, and of the *Annual Register* and its forerunner, have also an historical value. The journals of Parliament likewise contain in their bulky folios much that throws light on the past.

The library has a fair collection of English topography. The County Histories are yearly becoming more scarce and valuable. Of these we may name Surtees' Durham, Ormerod's Cheshire, Hutchin's Dorset, Whittaker's Richmondshire, Leeds, and Whalley, Clutterbuck's Hertfordshire, Shaw's Staffordshire, Eyton's Shropshire, Morant's Essex, Atkyn's Gloucestershire, Baines' Lancashire, Dugdale's Warwickshire and Monasticon, Polwhele's Devon, and Baker's Northamptonshire. This group alone represents a money value of about £350.

The collections respecting local history are very extensive, care having been taken to preserve not only large books but also those trifles which are sometimes of more importance to the historian. The pamphlet, the report, the broadside, which to-day is gladly given to all who care for it, at the end of a few years has become a rarity, and cannot be had. This class the library, with more or less of success, endeavours to preserve for future reference. Local newspapers come under this category, and of those published from about 1775 to the present time there is a very good collection.

The scientific section of the library varies considerably in the completeness of its respective subdivisions. Probably the best filled are those relating to botany and astronomy, though there are many important works on civil engineering and other branches. In botany we may name Blume's Plants of Java, Wallich's Asiatic Plants, Curtis's Flora Londinensis and Botanical Magazine, Sowerby's Botany, and Hooker's Ferns. These are all splendid specimens of book illustration in colours. The student of astronomy will find here not only the text books of that science, but valuable editions of the works of Galileo, Kepler, Delambre, Lagrange, and very many other important writers.

Lovers of the most scientific of amusements— Chess—will be glad to learn that a good corner has been reserved for treatises on that game. The books on shorthand are not so numerous as those at the

Chetham Library, but are still noticeable. They include a copy of Kopp's great work on ancient tachygraphy and the MS. collections for a history of shorthand, made by Mr. Harland. There are also several shorthand periodicals, including a set of the Phonetic Journal.

There are many fine works on architecture and the cognate arts. When the library opened the Prince Consort marked his sense of the importance of the work it was undertaking by sending as a donation the splendid books on ornament of Zahn and Gruner. Notable additions have been made to this class from time to time. Of these we must be content to name only—Du Sommerard on the Arts of the Middle Ages (worth £70), the Antiquities of the Russian Empire (worth £40), Letaroulley's Modern Rome, Viollet-le-Duc's Dictionary, a nearly complete collection of the writings of Ruskin, and a similar assemblage of the ornate works of Pugin.

Turning to general literature it is evident that in English literature, and especially poetry, the collection is a strong one. The editions of our standard authors include some very valuable issues of the seventeenth and eighteenth centuries. Although necessarily far less complete in foreign books, care has been taken to obtain some at least of the masterpieces of continental literature. If the more modern magicians are absent, Voltaire, Sainte Beuve, Chateaubriand, Goethe, Schiller, Heine, Camoens, Calderon, and other master spirits are present.

The classical department has been considerably

increased of late years. Besides the collections of Grævius and Gronovius, it includes Didot's edition of the Greek writers, and Valpy's issue of the Delphin Latin classics, and many rare and valuable editions of separate authors. We may perhaps here most fittingly name the Elzevir "Republics."

There are many long series of periodicals, amongst them the American Journal of Science and Arts (a nearly complete set of this, in England, rare and important magazine), Art Journal, Athenæum, Atlantic Monthly, Bibliotheca Sacra (rare in this country), Blackwood, Bookseller, British Almanac, British Quarterly Review, Builder, Chambers's Journal, Chemical News, Contemporary Review, Cornhill, Dublin Review, Economist, Edinburgh Review, Engineer, Fortnightly, Fraser's Magazine, Gentleman's Magazine (a complete set from the beginning in 1732), Herald and Genealogist, Inquirer, John Bull, Lancet, the Philosophical Magazine (a nearly complete set of this valuable periodical), London Quarterly, Macmillan's Magazine, Monthly Homœopathic Review, North American Review, Notes and Queries, Once a Week, Pharmaceutical Journal, Popular Science Review, Portfolio, Quarterly Journal of Science, Quarterly Review, Reliquary, Saturday Review, Scientific American, Spectator, Temple Bar, Theological Review, Trübner's American and Oriental Literary Record, Vanity Fair Album, Westminster Review, Zoologist, Bentley's Miscellany, Student and Intellectual Observer, North British Review, The Chronicle (1867-8 complete), Christian Observer, European Magazine, Andrew's Truth-teller, Fine Arts Quarterly, Hebrew Review, Autographic Mirror, Graphic, Illustrated London News, The Patrician, Christian Teacher, Prospective Review, Retrospective Review, Recreative Review, Classical Journal, Asiatic Journal, Mechanics' Magazine, Christian Reformer, Christian Reflector, Classical Museum, and English Review. In this list, lengthy as it is, we have only named those which are noticeable on account of the approximate completeness of the sets, or of the rarity of the journals. There are a few foreign periodicals of importance. The first place is due to the long set of the Journal des Economistes, containing the most important writings of the French statisticians and political economists since 1846. There are are also the Revue des deux Mondes, the Revue Celtique, the Rivista de España, the Rivista Europea, the Deutsche Rundschau, and Dingler's Journal. We may name also a small but very interesting collection of books, illustrative of some of the modern phases of spiritualism. Some of these, especially the smaller periodicals, are already rare.

There is a good working collection in bibliography. Books of this class are indispensable to those who have the management of a large library. Amongst them may be named a fine series of Dibdin's works, and an extensive collection of the writings of Quérard. The value of indexes of every kind leads us to mention the clue to the contents of the publications of societies issued by Reuss at the beginning of the century, and its successor (so far as science is concerned), the Catalogue of Scientific Papers issued by the Royal Society.

The library has an extensive collection of books

published by societies and printing clubs. Amongst
the printing societies we may name the Hakluyt,
Holbein, Shakspere, New Shakspere, Manx,
Spenser, Surtees, Harleian, Parker, Maitland, Percy,
Ballad, Historical Society of Science, Camden,
Chaucer, Early English Text, Chetham, Banna-
tyne. Sydenham, Spalding, Ecclesiastical His-
tory, Spottiswood, Ælfric, the Ray and English
Dialect Societies, the Smithsonian Institution, the
Warton Club, the Cobden Club, and the Oriental
Translation Fund. In this connection may be named
the numerous works issued by Mr. Grosart in his
Fuller's Worthy Library, and the serial publications
which have succeeded it. Amongst societies publish-
ing transactions or periodicals to be found in the
library are the Royal, the Chemical, the Asiatic, the
Agricultural, the Statistical, the Palæontographical,
the Geographical, the Horticultural, the Zoological,
the Anthropological, and the Aeronautical Societies.
Then there are the British Association, the Social
Science Association, the Archæological Institute,
the Archæological Association, the Iron and Steel
Institute, the Royal Institution, the Geological
Survey, the Royal Society of Literature, the Society
of Biblical Archæology, and the Society of
Arts. There are also a few colonial and American associations, e.g., the Royal Society of
Victoria. In this place we may most fittingly name the valuable publications issued by
or relating to the British Museum. These range
from lists of beetles to facsimiles of Egyptian papyri.
The immense series of photographs from the antiquities in the national collection are worthy of

special mention. In turning over these immense folios it is a matter of regret to remember that the pictures are as fleeting as they are faithful, and in another generation will probably have faded out of sight. The transactions of the local societies are of course well represented. There are the publications of the Sanitary Association, the Literary and Philosophical, the Geological, the Statistical, and the Numismatic Societies of Manchester ; the Historic Society of Lancashire and Cheshire, and the Literary and Philosophical Society of Liverpool. The reports of the Field Naturalists' Association, especially the latest issues, contain much that is noteworthy. We notice that the Chester Archæological Society is not represented in the library. For their publications a visit to Peel Park becomes necessary.

The works of reference strictly so called include the great French Encyclopédie, that of Chambers (both the ancient and the modern) the Britannica, Penny, English, and others. There are the dictionaries of Dr. William Smith, Biblical dictionaries of Kitto and Alexander, various biographical dictionaries old and new, directories, law lists, calendars, and the like, amongst them hundreds of dreary volumes which would be scorned even on a wet day and yet which are of the highest importance sometimes when we are in search of the particular piece of information which they alone can impart.

XVIII.

THE FREE LENDING LIBRARIES.

The lending departments of the Manchester Free Library will not be expected to present any very special feature to the notice of the bibliographer. The Campfield Lending Library as the oldest has, however, in process of time acquired some books of a character not usually found in collections destined chiefly for popular use. Amongst these we may name a goodly number of periodicals such as the Gentleman's Magazine, the Monthly Review, and so forth. In travels, also, the collection is very far from being contemptible. The duty of providing for all tastes necessarily prevents the lending libraries from attaining more than a rudimentary position. This is not in any sense a reflection upon their power for good. It is true that upon even the minutest topic there has been that making of many books which is a weariness to the flesh, but fortunately the gist of them so far as the general reader need trouble can be condensed into comparatively small compass. The lending libraries can therefore be made to represent much more completely than might be thought possible the encyclopædic aspects of human knowledge. Thus, if we take the youngest of these libraries—that at Cheetham—it will be found to contain something upon most of the prominent objects of literary and scientific interest. Whether the inquirer wants to know about bells or pottery, how to play chess or how to cook a dinner, he will find books available for the purpose. He will also find the writings of most of those great spirits who as poets or philosophers have left a legacy to the present generation. There is also a taste of foreign literature which may be of service to those who, having " learned " a language, want to find out something about it. In theology the broader divisions of thought are carefully presented.

One pleasing feature should not go unnamed. The musical taste of the Lancashire people has long been a matter of note. The managers of the lending libraries have therefore done well in providing a liberal supply of the best musical compositions. The works of Bach, Beethoven, Handel, Haydn, Mozart, Meyerbeer, and others of more recent date will help to keep alive and elevate this taste.

The Hulme Lending Library a few years ago, received a legacy of £100 bequeathed to it by the late Mr. James Gaskill, a man dear to all who knew him, and honourably distinguished for his advocacy of education and social reform. The Government having mulcted the institution of £10 for " legacy duty " the remainder was expended in the purchase of works chiefly of a scientific character. The books thus bought relate to the mechanical arts, architecture, the fine arts, music, music, astronomy, natural philosophy, physical geography, geology, chemistry, metallurgy, natural history, botany, entomology, zoology, anatomy, and physiology, mental science, medicine, microscopy, philosophy, history of law, anthropology, philology, geography, and history. The Gaskill bequest has been most wisely expended, and the literature purchased with it may in the future stimulate to exertion intellectual powers that might otherwise remain dormant.

The object kept in view in the formation of the lending libraries has been that of providing for more popular uses than are catered for in the Reference Library. They offer at least the elements of knowledge in every branch of learning, and the great masters of thought and poetry. They cannot exhaust any domain of investigation, but they can give to the youth fresh from school access to the best literature of his own country, and to a selection either in the originals or in translations of that which is important in the writings of other countries. They can also give the elements of scientific information, and something more than the elements of historical knowledge. As in all libraries intended for really popular use, there is a considerable quantity of fiction in these lending libraries. At its lowest the lending library responds to a legitimate desire for amusement; at its highest it may serve to inspire an ardour of investigation, and afford valuable help in the formation of character, and of a right method of conduct of the life. The extent of the free lending system may be estimated from the fact that the six libraries contain an aggregate of 79,066 volumes, distributed thus:— Campfield, 18,532; Hulme, 13,670; Ancoats, 12,473; Rochdale Road, 13,221; Chorlton and Ardwick, 13,426; Cheetham, 7,744. There have been catalogues published of each of these collections, arranged on the "Index plan" introduced into England by Dr. Crestadoro, and which from its elasticity and usefulness is fast superseding other forms of cataloguing for popular use.

XIX.

THE OVERSEERS' LIBRARY.

The most interesting, from a local point of view, of the many minor libraries of the city is the small but valuable collection belonging to the Overseers of the Poor. It does not contain many more than 400 volumes, but every book has a specific value and use, and the bulk of the collection refers to the history of the district, and contains material of great importance for the right understanding of the past. The general collection does not call for any very detailed notice. There are the voluminous reports of the Charity Commissioners, an enormous monument of the piety and occasionally of the well-meaning folly of our ancestors, and sometimes a record of the varied ways in which the grasp of the dead hand has been eluded and the intentions of the pious founder frustrated, not by the application of the endowment to useful purposes, but by its misappropriation by private greed. Of how many "lost charities" these volumes speak! There are, of course, books relating to the history of the poor, and to the mechanism by which their "right to live" is acknowledged. There are good editions of some of the English poets. The lover of finely-illustrated works will find a beautiful copy of Reveil's Museum of Painting and Sculpture, extending to seventeen volumes, with the text in French and English. He will find also Roberts's Holy Land, Westwood's Palæographia Sacra, and some others of a similar kind. Especially should he notice those beautiful examples of Bewick's powers—the Select Fables and the British Birds. Amongst the older books is a copy of George Sandy's Travels (1610).

The chief interest then centres in the part of the collection which refers to the political, social, and municipal history of Manchester. There are many of the pamphlets and small books relating to the intense political excitement which appears to have been chronic in the town at the commencement of the century. The troubles which befel Mr. Thomas Walker, the boroughreeve, can be fully traced, and there are ample materials for the study of the dismal tragedy of Peterloo. There are most of the celebrated political trials of the period. Nor are the darker shades wanting. Manchester has at times had "distinguished" performers in "murder considered as a fine art," and the record of their ghastly doings will be found amongst these tracts. There are many others of a very varied and miscellaneous character. We may name amongst the local books the Foundations of Manchester, Byrom's Poems, 1773; Manchester Vindicated, 1749; and Clayton's Advice to the Poor of Manchester, with the curious sequel by J. Stot, cobbler. The last two are simply pamphlets. Another of this class is an amusing satire on the old yeomanry. It is entitled "The Eight Days' Diary of a Member of the Yeomanry Cavalry during permanent duty. By Squib. Manchester, 1820." The interest of this particular copy is that Mr. F. R. Atkinson

has supplied the real names of most of the person-
ages who masquerade in Squib's diary from
Major Grim (ι e. Birley) downwards.   Another
thin volume contains Seddon's satirical portraits of Manchester public men of the last century,
and also a copy of the Poetical Correspondent or
Sketches of Manchester in verse. Manchester, 1767.
Of this rare tract Mr. Harland has given a description in his Collectanea. A rare work is " Clerimont,
or Memoirs of the Life and Adventures of Mr.
B * * *, written by himself.   Interspersed with
original anecdotes of living characters. Liverpool :
Printed by Charles Woseneraft, 1786." The preface
is signed with the initials C. W. B., and the writer
claims to be the descendant of one of the regicides,
and also of a minister in Bolton who for his own
benevolence and the zeal with which he stimu-
lated that of others was said to be " the boldest
beggar" in that town.   Clerimont is dedicated
to oblivion, and has safely reached its address.

We now come to the scrap-books, in which the
strength of the collection lies. No. 354 is a volume
entitled Portraits, Old Halls, and Antiquities illustrative of Lancashire.   The title-page is a design
by Mr. Jesse Lee, of Hulme, and is dated 1836.
Whether the volume was made by him or by Mr.
F. R. Atkinson is not very clear. It contains some
of the neat but peculiar handwriting of the last-
named gentleman, and has also inserted in it autographs of John Philip Kemble, Dr. Thomas
Percival, and others. One of the most striking
things in it is a portrait of Mr. Sylvanus Hibbert,
who had queer views on the subject of death and

immortality, and gave them to the world in a pamphlet, now of excessive rarity.

> Bury me not, for Heaven's sake,
>   In hopes that I must rise;
> If that's the object of my wish,
>   Why not now mount the skies.

This is a suggestion that is certainly pertinent, if not practical. It does not appear that Mr. Hibbert carried out these aspirations. The face is one full of quaint character, as shown in this portrait. There is a small collection of street ballads, varying in probable date throughout the present century. One of them is a political strain by the "revered and ruptured Ogden." He was the son of that writer of dull doggerel known as "Poet Ogden," and having imbibed liberal opinions, found his way against his will into Horsemonger Gaol. His treatment there led to a debate in the House of Commons, in which Canning was accused, but unjustly, of using the revolting alliteration we have quoted. Another of these ballads refers to the last experiences of Mr. Thomas Armstrong, who was hung at Lancaster in 1817, for setting fire to a cotton mill with a view of obtaining the insurance money. There is a volume, lettered on the binding Manchester Scraps, and numbered No. 361. It is a wonderful farrago. There are broadsides of every imaginable description, requisitions to the boroughreeve for the holding of town's meetings, protests against the decisions of such assemblies, exposures of that "other side" which always does the naughty tricks, calendars of prisoners with the death penalty attached in ghastly frequency, programmes of fancy balls, sermons, and a hundred other varieties. There is a small quarto scrap-book (No. 330), which contains various portraits and caricatures, amongst them Joseph Brotherton, John Davies, the lecturer, and Thomas Battye, the energetic exposer of parochial abuses, several of whose tracts are in the collection. This volume contains also an ingenious quarto trade prospectus issued by Mr. W. M. Craig, the author and artist, who was at that time a writing-master at No. 6, St Mary's Gate. Pertaining to the same class is No. 409, " The Manchester and Lancashire Collector, a large folio volume containing a collection of Lacashire, antiquarian, local, and other cuttings, scraps, and MSS. engravings, plates, &c., put together by J. Harland, 1866." The volume contains 278 pages, or nearly 800 columns, of generally small type ; more than equal to twenty ordinary volumes. This contains a great number of Mr. Harland's own contributions to periodicals, interspersed with prints and pieces in manuscript.

The name of Thomas Barrett is one familiar to all readers about old Manchester. His industry must have been prodigious, for traces of him are found in many directions. The bulk of his MSS. are in the Chetham Library, but several of these scrap-books contain evidences of his industry alike with pen and pencil. No. 331 is a MS. catalogue of the Museum which he formed of stained glass, old armour, and miscellaneous antiquities. There are in it several of his drawings of archæological objects.

There are scrap-books formerly belonging to Mr.

John Greaves. These were lent to Mr. Edward Baines when he was engaged upon his History of Lancashire. They are particularly rich in matter relating to the amusements of the town. One of the first pages announces the performances here of that mysterious man-woman the Chevalière d'Eon ; then we have Bradbury performing the anvil trick, and tribes of giants and dwarfs, performing dogs, Indian savages, and all the rest of those who live by amusing their fellow-creatures. Then there are portraits of byegone local celebrities, " Limping Tom," " Patten Nat," " Old Chelsea Buns " and " Young Chelsea Buns," honest John Shaw, and scores of others. There are squibs against Joshua Brookes, rhymes against the Government, street ballads, and pictures of old places that have long since disappeared.

The last volume to which we need call attention is a volume of street ballads, which also comes from the Greaves collection. Those who love a " ballad i' print" will find here between seven and eight hundred of them, dating from the earlier part of the present century. They are of every conceivable class, patriotic—one sings of " Elba room for Boney"—amatory, comic, and disreputable. Some of these ballads have been for centuries the delight of the people. A few of them have reference to this locality, and celebrate the doings of "Th' Mon at Measter Grundy's," or chant the praises of the " Flower of Lancashire," or of the fair " Lancashire Witches." The volume contains also a few garlands. One of these relates the career of a modern Faust, " Mr. John Brennon," who sold his soul to the devil for eight years' enjoyment of

life.   There are instances of persons devoting themselves to the infernal deities for a smaller reward
than this.

The library is, of course, only a public library
from the circumstance that it is the property of a
public office.   The books have helped inquirers in
past times, and, we have no doubt, will be accessible
for any definite and legitimate purpose now.

XX.

UNITARIAN HOME MISSIONARY BOARD.

The Unitarian Home Missionary Board, which has its home in the Memorial Hall, Albert Square, is a strangely named Theological College. Its object is to train young men to act as home missionaries and ministers. For the purpose of aiding the work of the classes there is a library. It is, however, very small, and needs a good deal of filling up in every department before it can be held to represent in anything like an adequate degree the present condition of theological science. The sections devoted to general literature are very unimportant. There are few classics, a fine edition of Polydore Vergil de rerum Inventoribus (Basilae, 1525); a Latin volume of Herrara's Indias Occidentales (1622), and an edition of Polybius (Basilae, 1549).

We come now to examine the distinctly theological part of the collection—the printed editions of the text are not numerous, but there is a copy of the splendid edition of Codex Sinaiticus issued by the liberality of the Emperor Alexander. Amongst the aids to the acquisition of Hebrew is Udall's Key of the Holy Tongue (Leyden, 1593).

There is a fine folio series of the works of Socinus, Crellius, Schlichtingus, and Wolzogen. There are some of Biddle's tracts, and a great number of publications relating to the more modern phases of the Unitarian thought. It is curious to note however that of works relating to the Racovian Controversy there is a much finer collection in the Free Library than here.   The View of Popery, by Joseph Burroughs (2nd edit., 1737), contains an interesting reference to and engraving of the celebrated Pardon monument in Macclesfield church.

The library has recently been re-arranged, and the classification now adopted may be worth giving as one suitable for small theological libraries and easily modified to suit the special features of the book collection of different denominations.

I. Text of the Old and New Testament.

    a. Polyglots.
    b. Portions of Hebrew and Greek text.
    c. English, French, and other versions.
    d. Apocryphal books.

II. Aids to the Study of the Text.

    a. General and special introductions.
    b. Harmonies, abridgments, &c.
    c. Treatises on the history of the text and it versions.
    d. Dictionaries and Concordances.
    e. Aids to the study of Hebrew.
    f. Aids to the study of New Testament Greek.
    g. Commentaries.

III. Ritual and Ceremonial, Hebrew and Christian.

    a. Sacrifice.
    b. Sacraments.
    c. Councils.
    d. Canon Law.
    e. Church Government.

IV. History of the Church.

    a. General.

    b. The Jewish Church.

    c. Lives of Christ.

    d. History of the foundation of the Christian Church.

    e. History of the Church in various epochs.

    f. Lives of Saints.

    g. Lives of Popes.

    h. History of Missions.

    i. History of the Inquisition.

    j. History of Religious orders.

V. Christian Dogma and Controversy.

    a. The Fathers.

    b. Catechisms, Liturgies, Forms of Prayer.

    c. Sermons.

    d. Miscellaneous theology, treatises on the evidences of the Christian religion and on its dogmatic and moral teaching.

    e. Treatises on the Controversy between the Church of Rome and the Protestant Churches.

    f. Controversies between Church and Dissent in England.

    g. Socinian and Unitarian Controversy.

    h. Treatises on Toleration.

    i. Eccentric Sects.

    j. Writings of Mystics and Ascetics.

VI. Controversy between the opponents of Christianity and its defenders.

VII. Natural Theology.

VIII. Comparative Mythology and the History of
Religion.
  a. History of Religions.
  b. Greek and Roman Mythology.
  c. Mohammedanism.
  d. Buddhism.
  e. Paganism generally.

The library possesses only one MS., which was
presented by Mr. H. A. Bright, of Liverpool. It
is a collection of autograph letters of the Rev.
Theophilus Lindsey, extending from 1775 to 1800,
and relating to many interesting topics of theology
and critical learning. The library contains about
3,000 vols.

XXI.

ROYAL INFIRMARY.

The Royal Infirmary was established in 1754 and in 1791 the present library was commenced for the benefit of the medical staff. The books are for the most part allowed to circulate, with the exception of the more valuable works. The rules provide that the library shall be accessible from nine to nine. There are altogether about 3,000 volumes in the collection, which has been brought together with very definite practical views. The historical element of medical literature is not very strongly represented, but the practical part of it is extremely full. In some specialities, for instance, ophthalmology, the books are full and fine.

A catalogue has been printed with the following title :—

Classed Catalogue of Books in the Library of the Royal Infirmary, Manchester, 1859. Manchester: Printed by T. Sowler and Son, St. Ann's Square. 4to.

This was drawn up by Dr. Frank Renaud, and is arranged in the following classes :—Anatomy, Physiology, Botany, Chemistry, Medical Jurisprudence, Materia Medica, and Therapeutics, Pharmacy, Midwifery, Pathology, Practice of Physic, Surgery, Geology, Mineralogy and Meteorology, Natural History, Natural and Mechanical Philosophy, Transactions and Periodicals, Dictionaries and Cyclopædias, Catalogues, Medical Biography and Literature, Miscellaneous and General Literature.

There are comparatively few of the older books.

Amongst them may be named volumes of Glauber, Dodonæus, and Libavii Alchemia (1597, 4to).

The most interesting section of the library to a non-professional person is the portion devoted to illustrated books. Of these there are several fine ones. Splendid examples of artistic work are the folios of Caldani, Icones Anatomicæ, printed at Venice in 1801, Cloquet's Anatomie de l'Homme (Paris, 1821); Tiedemann's Tabulæ Arteriarum (Carlsruhe, 1822); and the volumes of plates bearing the names of Camper, Smellie, Astley Cooper, Haller, Bell, William Hunter, and others. Cowper's Anatomy of Humane Bodies, printed in 1737, contains some beautiful specimens of the engraver's art. Later we may name Bourgery. On the confines of medical science we have Russell's Indian Serpents (1796), with its careful portraits of those beautiful but unattractive creatures. Cruvelhier's Anatomie Pathologique (1829-35) is a work well known for its importance and excellence. There is also a work by Lebert on the same subject. The student of skin diseases will find much to interest him in the great work of Alibert (showing cases brought into the Hospital St. Louis), with its quaint frontispiece looking like a genealogical table, but labelled "Arbre des Dermatoses." Another important work in this class is that by Cazenave. There is a grotesqueness approaching the ludicrous in some of these faithful pictorial statements of the ravages which disease occasionally makes in the human face divine. The troubles to which the eye is subject are shown in the wonderful work of Ruete.

The books relating to the history of medical science are not very numerous. There is Leclerq's Histoire de la Médicine Arabe (1866). There is also the translation of the matter attributed to the Welsh Physicians of Myddvai, published by the Welsh MSS. Society. This contains of course a large proportion of charms and superstitious usages. One saying in it avers that "he who sees fennel and gathers it not, is not a man but a devil;" another that "he who goes to sleep supperless will have no need of Rhiwallon of Myddvai"—the physician. Whatever may be thought of these statements the sentiment that "God sends food to washed hands" is highly to be commended. Apart from its theological probability, it has an immediate sanitary value.

XXII.

THE SCHILLER ANSTALT.

This institution owes its origin to the enthusiasm
excited by the Schiller Centenary Festival of 1859.
It is a foreign clubhouse with the addition of literary
attractions not always associated with the club
whether native or foreign. The library is not very
large, nor does it offer very many special features of
interest It is in the main a collection of German
authors in serviceable editions. The books are good
and likely to be of use but not remarkable from a
bibliographical point of view. The class of "collected
works" range from Byron to Luther The "Dictionaries, Encyclopædies, and works on Philology" are
not numerous. It is strange that no library in Manchester has a copy of Ersch and Gruber's great
encyclopædia. Works on Philosophy, Theology,
Church History, and "Padagogik" form another
class, of which the Greek Testament, Plato, Spinosa,
Strauss, and Schopenhauer form portions. The
section of "Political Economy, Law, Art of War,
Trade and Manufactures" includes "Der neue
Pitaval," thirty-four volumes devoted to the history
of celebrated crimes, some committed by and others
on the persons commemorated. The next classes
are "Natural Science, Medicine, and Mathematics,"
and "Geography and Travels." In "History,
Archæology, and Mythology" we may name a long
series of Raumer's Historisches Taschenbuch. After
the section of "Biography and Correspondence," we

have "History of Literature and Culture," which ranges from Hagen's Minnesinger to Noël's "Leçons Françaises." The books on Æsthetics and Art history include Kugler, Lubke, Waagen and Winckelmann. There are many "Poetical and Dramatic works," and more "Romances and Novels." The "Miscellaneous" section includes Bettina's suppositious Correspondence with Goethe, almanacks directories, books on phrenology, chess, &c. There are a few Periodicals and an interesting collection of "Flugschriften" on politics, literature, art, and all the other multitudinous subjects on which pamphlets can be written. There is a printed list of the books, classified as above indicated :—

Katalog der Bibliothek der Manchester Schiller Anstalt. Leipzig druck von Fischer and W. Hig. 1867. 8vo. pp. 115.

There has been a lithographed supplement to this catalogue :—

Anhang zum Katalog der Bibliothek der Schiller Anstalt in Manchester. F. Bedkober, lithographer and printer, 91, Market Place, Manchester. 8vo. pp. 28.

XXIII.

THE FOREIGN LIBRARY.

The Foreign Library was instituted February 3, 1830. It is a subscription library of the old type, but the books are purchased " as nearly in the following proportion and value as circumstances will permit, viz : two-fifths French, two-fifths German, one-fifth Italian." A few Spanish works may be added occasionally. The cost of a share is one guinea, with an annual subscription of one and a-half guinea. The library has been more than once catalogued :—

Catalogue of the Manchester Foreign Library (established February 3, 1830) for German, French, Italian, and Spanish Books. 1868. Compiled by C. Frederick Schmidt, Manchester, 1868. 8vo.

A good notion of the scope of the library may be gathered from the names occurring in that section of this catalogue, which contain the " collective works." This includes the names of Andrieux, Arago, Balzac, Bentham, Beranger, Castelli, Chamisso, Claudius, Corneille, Courier, Destouches, Fichte, Forster, Goethe, Gotthelf (= Bitzius), Gresset, Hauff, Heine, Herder, W. von Humboldt, Kleist, Klinger, Klopstock, Körner, Kotzebue, Lessing, Lichtenberg, Machiavelli, Moliere, Montesquieu, Moser, W. Muller, Novalis, Oehlenschlager, Pfaff, Racine, Raimund, Regnard, Fritz Reuter, Richter, Rousseau, Saphir, Schiller, Ernst Schulze, Seume, Van der Velde, Voltaire, Wieland, and

Zschokke. This is a mixture of great and little, wit and heaviness but fairly represents the breadth of the remaining classes. The classification is as follows :—

I. Collective Works.
II. Philosophy, Education.
III. Physics, Natural History.
IV. Geography, Voyages, and Travels.
V. History, Biography, Letters, and Correspondence.
VI. History of Literature and Civilization.
VII. Fine Arts, History of Arts, Æsthetics.
VIII. Dictionaries, Encyclopædias, Language.
IX. Romances, Novels, Polite Literature.
X. Poetry and the Drama.
XI. Theology, Mythology.
XII. Politics, Jurisprudence.
XIII. Periodical Publications.

We can only name a few of the books :—Buffon (Paris, 1799, in 74 vols.) ; Raumer's Historisches Taschenbuch ; Ferrario's Bibliografia dei romanzi e poemi romanzeschi d'Italia (1818) ; Rèpertoire dramatique de Scène Française (40 vols.) ; Hitzig and Haering, Der neue Pitaval. The periodicals include many volumes of the Revue Encyclopédique, Revue des deux Mondes, Das Ausland, and others.

The catalogue is very carefully compiled, and only lacks an index of subjects. Three supplements have been issued, making a complete record of the eleven thousand volumes now in the library.

XXIV.

THE LAW LIBRARY.

The Law Library dates from 1820. It is a strictly professional collection, nor would the general readers be greatly tempted by the literature it contains. Law is like science, always changing, though whether like science it always moves in a progressive spirit, may sometimes be a matter of doubt. The great works of literature last for centuries undimmed, but a masterly exposition of the law of some particular subject may be rendered obsolete by the parliamentary wisdom of next session. The intricate confusion of our uncodified laws, the clashing caused by the contradictory systems at work in the different sections of the United Kingdom, and the continual tinkering to which the statute book is condemned by parliamentary action make a library of this kind almost indispensable to members of the legal profession. The books are arranged in nine classes. A. Reports of Cases. B Civil, Colonial, Foreign, International, Irish, Isle of Man, and Scotch Law, Foreigners in Great Britain. C. Constitutional Law, Legal History, Science and Study, General Abridgments and Digests of Law and Equity. D. Criminal, Crown, Magisterial, Municipal, Parliamentary, and Parochial Law. E. Debtor and Creditor, Maritime, Mercantile, and Military Law, Personal Property. F. Equity, Real Property. G. Common Law, Ecclesiastical Law, Courts of a Special Jurisdiction. H Maps and

Plans, Parliamentary and Public Documents and Records, Statutes. I. Digests and Indexes to Reported Cases, Legal Periodicals, Miscellaneous Subjects, and General Literature. This classification can only be regarded as a rough method of bringing together books on cognate topics. It has no philosophical basis nor is there any thread of continuity visible in the arrangement. There is a good list of the books :—

> Catalogue of books of the Manchester Law Library Society, instituted July 21st, 1820. 1869. Manchester: Cave and Sever, 1869. 8vo.

> Manchester Law Library Society, Addenda to the catalogue of 1869. November, 1874. Manchester: Cave and Sever, 1874, 8vo.

The titles are arranged alphabetically by the author's names, and an excellent index of subjects enables the consultor to learn without difficulty what the library can offer in the way of separate treatises on the matter he has in hand. If he wants to imitate Thelusson, by consulting the books named under the head Accumulation, he may see how far the law will allow to go in having money at interest after his death ; if a sporting man, under "Horses," he will find a book on the law of races, wagers, &c. There are a large number of private acts relating to Manchester and the neighbourhood. There do not appear to be many books relating to law considered as a science, or in its relation to the history of culture and civilization.

XXV.

THE RADFORD LIBRARY AT ST. MARY'S HOSPITAL.

This library is the result of the individual liberality of its founder, Dr. Thomas Radford. After many years of intimate and honourable connection with St. Mary's Hospital, he transferred to that institution his own valuable collection of books, and further provided for its endowment. The trustees appointed were Messrs. Herbert Birley, Arthur Heywood, and Robert Gladstone, the last named since deceased. Dr. Radford has also presented his valuable obstetrical Museum to St. Mary's Hospital. The books naturally reflect the special studies of the collector. It is a capital library of obstetrical literature, and of books relating to the diseases of women and children. German writers are but sparingly represented, but the English and French authors very fully. The books are not confined to the classes named, though undoubtedly those are the most prominent sections. There are many periodicals, and of these Dr. Radford with wise liberality supplies the continuations. In the same manner he makes additions of new and important treatises. Amongst the illustrated books the fine folios of Caldani may be named. There is an interesting edition of Guido de Chauliac, followed by the treatises of Lanfranc, Bertapalia, and others (1512). There is here the fine folio of the works of Avicenna printed at Basle in 1566. Of the other large books we may name the best edition of Sanchez de Matrimonio (1608), with its singular passages on delicate subjects, the English translation of the works of Glauber (1689), and the collection of treatises issued under the title Gynaeciorum libri (1576, 4 vols.). This last has once been the property of J. V. C. Moehsen, a Berlin M.D. of the last century, and his bookplate, which is larger than this page contains both his own portrait and a view of his library. Another is a presentation copy with the author's autograph inscription to Dr. Radford of Naegele's Schräg-verengte Becken (1839).

There are a few MSS. but they are all modern and comparatively unimportant, consisting chiefly of lectures, notes, essays, and similar exercises.

One of the earlier books is a copy of the " Byrth of Mankinde, otherwise named the Woman's Book, set foorth in English by Thomas Raynalde." This edition was printed in 1598. The edition of 1540 is said to be one of the earliest examples of the use of copperplate engraving in this country.

Palfyn's " Description Anatomique " (1708) may be named for the sake of its very curious " Traité des Monstres." These are forms of abnormal ugliness and grotesque distortion, highly creditable to the imagination of the artist.

The collection is rich in pamphlet literature. Of the importance of these ephemeral productions we need not speak. There are many volumes of these tracts, monographs on special points of medical treatment, records of cases, documents relating to dead and buried quarrels, exposures, justifications, answers, replies, rejoinders, and so forth. The rarest of the pamphlets is one that in its day served in place of a newspaper, and filled many households with wonder in the same way that some years ago all England was speculating on the case of the Welsh Fasting Girl. Yellow with age now are the dozen pages that set forth "A Notable and prodigious Historie of a Mayden, who for sundry yeeres neither eateth, drinketh, nor sleepeth." This tract having been set forth in "high Dutch" and in French, was translated into English and printed by John Woolfe in the year 1589. The name of the Fasting Maid was Katerin Cooper, and she lived at Schmidweiler, and successfully eluded the vigilance of the persons sent to examine into the truth of her case in 1584, when she 27 years of age. What was the end of Katerin Cooper? Did she die of starvation or amend her ways and fulfil the commonplace duties of a peasant's home? On these points the record is silent.

Mr. C. J. Cullingworth has for some time been engaged on the preparation of a catalogue, and we are glad to know that the library will soon have an adequate key to its varied and important contents.

XXVI.

AN HISTORICAL EPILOGUE.

In the course of this volume the most important of the existing Manchester libraries have been described. Many others exist which do not call for special description. In conclusion, some notes may be given of the general history of our public libraries.

No doubt the clergy of the Old Church, in their quaint home in the erewhile Baron's Hall would have a library, but we know of only one book which it may have contained.

The first public library of the district has an ecclesiastical flavour about it. Readers of the diary of that "godly puritan," Henry Newcome, will recollect his references to the "English Library." This was a bequest made by John Prestwych, B.D., some of whose divinity books were placed in the Jesus Chapel about 1653, for the benefit of the inhabitants. Chetham was one of Prestwych's trustees, and it might have been conjectured that it suggested the thought to him of founding the noble library by which his name has become dear to every scholar. At the date named, however, his own will was already made. This contained not only the provision for the foundation of the library, but also a legacy of £200 for the purchase of "godly books" to be placed in the churches of Manchester and Bolton, and the chapels of Turton, Walmsley, and Gorton. Those at Manchester appear to have been added to Prestwych's books, and to have been jointly styled the English Library. What use was made of them would now be hard to tell. The grave writings of Master Perkins may have had an effect upon the lives of those who read them chained to a pillar in the Parish Church, but no record remains of their operations. The band of silent monitors preaching a stern morality as well as a rigid piety may have kept some in the right path amid the debaucheries and temptations of the second Stuart period. Of much greater importance was the foundation of the Chetham Library. The liberality of the founder, seconded by the learning of those who had the primary management, produced a collection of lasting importance. Of course it is marked by the spirit of the age, and reflects in its earlier portions the weighty subjects upon which the thoughts of mankind were then busy. That a certain portion of the books should now have lost vital interest is not astonishing. There is this, however, about all books, that when they have ceased to be living forces capable of influencing human action, they still retain a documentary value as marking certain stages in the history of thought. The development of the Chetham Library has been stunted by want of funds. Whilst the estates of the hospital have flourished and increased greatly in value, those of the library have remained stationary, or actually receded. This has arisen, not from want of care in the management, but from the accident of their position.

The estates from which the revenues of the library are derived happen to be situated in localities untouched by the modern changes which have so greatly increased the value of real property in most parts of Lancashire. This has prevented the library keeping pace with the increase of modern literature. After making every deduction, however, the foundation of Humphrey Chetham is one of great usefulness and importance. It is to be hoped that some plan may be devised, not only for its maintenance, but for its increase and extension.

Akin to the Church libraries founded by Chetham was the bequest made to " Salford Chapel " by Humphrey Oldfield. The influence of such a small collection of books, even supposing them to have been much used by the congregation, could only be of a restricted nature.

For half a century there is a blank in our bibliothecal history. The official records of the old Subscription Library did not extend further back than 1765, but it may have existed some years earlier in a chrysalis state. This subscription library, with various changes of abode and management, was after an existence of a century dissolved by the consent of the proprietors, and the books sold by auction in 1867. It is to be regretted that when the difficulty of carrying on the library became apparent steps were not, taken to secure the collection for one of the other existing libraries. A century of growth must inevitably have brought together much that could not be readily acquired in the present day. The large collection of tracts went in a great measure to swell the extensive series of pamphlet volumes in the Free Library. Even in its palmy days the old Subscription Library did not fully supply the wants of the town. The "Jacobin" Library of 1792 still survives, apparently as vigorous as when it afforded the friends of progress the means of culture and refinement. The Portico which began in 1806 represents the subscription library with the addition of a certain club element in a rudimentary form. Various modifications of the subscription libraries are found in vogue in the first half of this century. Booksellers lent out their wares for hire, and some of these collections were far from being contemptible. Many representatives of this class still survive, but at present they are chiefly imitations on a small scale of Mudie and Smith. In the poorer districts they may help lads to volumes of more pronounced flavour than they could obtain from the Free Lending Libraries. Doubtless these proprietary libraries have been chiefly used for the dissemination of fiction. The taste for novel reading is not a thing of to-day. But if the circulating libraries of Bancks, Gray, Thomson, Campion, Ashworth, Leggatt, and others have probably circulated a good deal of rubbish, they will also have helped to popularize the best imaginative writing of the language. They may have lent out the inane romances of the Minerva Press, but they must have lent out the writings of Smollett, Fielding, and Scott. Some of the libraries contained matter of a more solid character. Certainly the most remarkable of them was the library of the Bible Christian Church in Salford. The books of the Rev. William Cowherd, with sundry additions, were used as a circulating library and as an adjunct of the educational work which the sect was then carrying on in its old home in the King-street "Academy."

This collection contained much that was curious and important in science and theology.

The Literary and Philosophical Society was organized in 1780, but its library did not attain any great importance for many years after. This is a type of library which does not appear to have flourished to the extent that might have been expected. The library of the Literary and Philosophical Society, although valuable, is partial in its development, and represents a view of science hardly wide enough for the present day.

From general science we may pass to the group representing professional studies. The Law Library commenced in 1820 with the laudable object of enabling its subscribers to master the shifting intricacies of English jurisprudence. A collection of this kind is doubly useful alike from the costly character of the books and from the kaleidoscopic rapidity with which changes are effected alike in principle and practice.

The Medical Library was commenced in 1834, and has now developed into a collection, remarkable in character and extent. It has survived many vicissitudes, and has, it may be hoped, a long and prosperous career before it.

The absence of a special theological library may perhaps be thought remarkable. The students of the Anglican Church perhaps have found sufficient for their wants in the Chetham Library. The want of any training college in the district may have led to the defect not being so much noticed. The Lancashire Independent College, founded in 1842, is a good type of the institutions by which

Dissenters have secured a liberal education for their ministry. Other vehicles for the diffusion of theological literature are furnished by the church, chapel, and Sunday school libraries. The Friends Library forms a good type of this first class. The number of volumes belonging to these religious collections is very great. No Sunday school is without a library of some sort. Their chief object is to afford moral instructions for the conduct of life and to show the grounds of dogma and the historical associations of the sect.

In 1826 the attempt to popularize science and knowledge led to the formation of the Mechanics' Institution. The library has had a fair development, but not perhaps to so great an extent as the educational departments. Nine years later the Athenæum was founded for a somewhat higher social grade.

The Corporation Library, which began in 1844, was a curious instance of a partial appreciation of a municipal duty followed by almost instant arrest of progress. The founders seem clearly to have seen that it is a legitimate function of a municipality to provide a library for the citizens. The collection was intended primarily for the use of the town council and officials, but in a secondary degree as a reference collection for the inhabitants. The inquiries which were made in 1849 into the provision of public libraries in various countries had an immediate effect in this district. Although the Chetham bequest was the first entirely free library in Europe, the provision of public libraries proceeded with much greater rapidity abroad than at home. The Chetham remained the solitary library of its class, and was also closed at those hours when an industrial population could alone make use of it. Perhaps in the course of the inquiry sufficient stress was not laid upon the activity of the influences which were spreading knowledge here, and which were not at work in countries containing more libraries. Many of the Continental collections were more antiquarian curiosities than anything else. There can, however, be no doubt that England compared very unfavourably with other States in the matter of public libraries. The inquiry served as a stimulus to action. One of its effects was to secure the passage of the Free Libraries Act. This has been productive of great good. Corporations already possessed a common law right to found such libraries, and that without the restrictions as to the amount to be expended. The corporations of London and of Bristol had libraries centuries before the passing of the statute, which authorizes the library rate. Whilst the bill was still being debated the Salford Free Library was formed, and after its passage the first place to make use of its machinery was Manchester. The opening of these free libraries marks a new departure. They bring the possibility of culture to the poorest. They are accessible at hours when the working classes are free from daily toil. The books represent a wide range of science, and exhibit that which is best in the literature not only of our own but of many lands. The action of the school boards in spreading popular education will no doubt make the younger generation better able to avail themselves of the facilities of free libraries. It should, however, be remembered that these libraries, maintained as they are by the public rates, are intended not for the use of any one class, but every section of the community. Since the establishment of the town libraries there has been only one further development which need be noticed, that is the Owens College Library, which from comparative insignificance, attained importance by the bequest of Bishop Lee. The future university has now an excellent nucleus of books.

The public libraries of Manchester and Salford are more numerous than is generally supposed, and for the most part they are administered in a wise and liberal spirit. The public press sometimes contains fallacious statistics as to the number of volumes in public libraries in relation to population. According to this often-repeated statement the public and large private libraries of Great Britain contain only 6 volumes to every 100 persons, whilst Bavaria is credited with $26\frac{1}{2}$ volumes. The public libraries of Manchester and Salford contain not less than 80 volumes for every hundred of the population. The books in them are fresher and have a greater educational value than those in some of the Continental libraries, which have been built up from the ruins of the monastic establishments. These may have more interest for the bibliomaniac, but will certainly be of less use in imparting knowledge and fitting their readers for the battle of life. As regards the free libraries great as has been their usefulness in the past, it can only be regarded as a dim prophecy of what is before them. Their sphere of action has been restricted by the want of elementary education. Those who can barely spell through a newspaper paragraph will not prove very appreciative students of Shakspere or Milton. With the greater diffusion of education we shall have an increased and increasing class able to avail themselves of the facilities for higher self-education, which libraries afford.

Ano gre ch · cc̄ · xlv · qui de clicis ipi
ur lef fct est
est annus regni Regis h̄ · die nat
xr ir · fuit idem Rex ad Natale dn̄i
londoñ · ibiq; die natalis Johem de ga
resdene clicum ⁊ multis duratu bñfi
cus · s; omib; au expectatum resignati ·
balteo cinct militari · ad coniugale
uitā qm p elegit conuolantes · Dieb;
sub eisdem elec cant ⁊ Wigorn ⁊ hefor
densis epi transferentur; qui int oms
anglie plator erant dn̄o ip specialissimi
⁊ ad uoluntatē ei pficienda ⁊ in detmētu
regni qi ipe eos creauit pmores · Elec
tiquidem cant naues ascēsur · iussie ne
iora archiepar ab scdir uendi ⁊ qual
dem tallias ⁊ collectas i tris suis fieri · Et
cōstituit qdam suu officialem ula̅ de
pictauenie magrm hugone de mor
temer · qi diligent mandata sua exeq
batur · De uero scā marcell; Regina
alienora peperit dn̄o Regi filium · Et
uocarum est nom ei aedmund · In
crastino ü purificanis be marie obiit co
mitissa gronie isabella de bolebec · Et
in crastino scī Valentini · obiit Balde
win comes deuonie adolescens primo
indol ⁊ miles elegantissim̄ · qm comi
te de insula de Witch uulgarit appella

Cy commence la premiere partie
de Valerius maxime du proesme
Vbis Rome ce translatement le com
cement du proesme de ce liure. Por
lentendement du quel auoir il est
a sauoir que Vincent en son miroeur hysto
rial Et plusieurs autres dient que Valere
fut ou temps de octouien. Mais suppose q ce
soit Vray toutesforz estoit il son liure du
temps de tybere cesaires qui apres octeuie
fut empereur sans nul moyen Et ceste
conclusion que ie tiens pour assez ferme sera
plus assez declairee et lieu ou il cheoza apres
Et les Rasons que semblent contraires
solutes bien clerement. presuppose doncqs q
Valerius feust du tempe de tybere cesaires au
moins quil escript son liure en son tempe car
il pourroit estre quil fut du temps octouian
Et quil escripst son liure du temps de tybere
ie vient a la translacion du proesent qui

Aynt Bartilmeð
thapostle wente in to
ynde/which is in thenð
te of the worlð / Andð
therin he entryðð in to
a Temple/where an I
doll was/which was nameðð Astaroth

DAVID GARRICK.

La premiere chose qu'on doit faire quand on a
emprunté un livre, c'est de le lire afin de pouvoir le rendre plutôt.

Menagiana: Vol IV.

William Shakspeare

Byrom

Delambre

F. Arago

Suum cuiqs.
Tho. Hearne
June 13 - 1722.

APPENDIX.

FIRST BOOK PRINTED IN MANCHESTER.

[The following is chiefly reprinted from Notes and Queries 4th S. iii. 97 and 4th vii. 64]:—

Some day, let us hope, the literary history of the cotton metropolis will be written; there is much more interest attaching to it than might perhaps at first be imagined. For instance, George Nicholson, one of her printers, may be said to be the originator of a cheap literature that was the reverse of cheap and nasty. Imison was one of the last of the old wood-engravers, and Nicholson employed Bewick, who raised that art from its fallen and degraded condition. R. and W. Dean followed close in Nicholson's steps, and Gleave took advantage of the book-hawking system to scatter over Lancashire the Bible and *Josephus*, and *Henry Earl of Moreland*, and many other works, which by no other plan could have reached the classes who thus acquired them. When the chronicler arises to do for Manchester what Mr. Robert Davies has done so well for York in his *Memorials of the York Press*, we may expect a curious and entertaining volume. In the meantime I wish to make a note on one subject which must receive the consideration of any one attempting the task.

At what date was printing first introduced into Manchester? In the first series of Archdeacon Cotton's *Typographical Gazetteer* we are told that it occurred in 1732 ; in the second series the date given is 1729. Neither of these dates is correct. Archdeacon Cotton's book carries such authority with it, that it is highly desirable that any omissions or mistakes in it should be pointed out, lest the errors become perpetuated.

The first *printing-press* that Manchester can boast was at work in the year 1587-8, but whether any book was actually issued from the Martin Marprelate press which had wandered to Newton Lane, is doubtful. The Earl of Derby seized the press, and though Waldegrave escaped, several of his men were taken. In Strype's *Annals of the Reformation* (Oxford, 1824, vol. iii. pt. 11. p. 602) is "The examination of divers persons about the printing-press of Martin Marprelate: and of the books so printed. Feb. 15, 1588, apud Lambhith in com. Surr."; from which the following passage is copied :—

"Hodgkins, and Symms, and Tomlyn, Hodgkin's men, confess, that beginning to print the book called *More Work for the Cooper*, in Newton-lane, near Manchester, they had printed thereof about six a quire of one side before they were apprehended. They also deposed that Hodgkins told them the next book, or the next but one, which they had to print, should be in Latin [which perhaps was *Disciplina Sacra*] ; and that there was another parcel of *More Work, &c.*, which should serve them to print another time : for this was but the first part of the said book : and the other part was almost as big again."

Perhaps the unlucky fate of these first printers may have deterred others of the fraternity from visiting Manchester. In 1661 we hear of a bookseller in Manchester who published—

"A Sermon preached at the Collegiate Church, Manchester, on Tuesday, the 23rd of April, 1661, being the Coronation Day of his Royal Majesty Charles II., by Richard Heyrick, Warden of the said College. London : Printed for Ralph Shelmerdine, Bookseller in Manchester, 1661."

This book is so rare—

"that, when the late Dr. Hibbert Ware was writing the *History of the Foundations of Manchester*, the publishers of that work advertised all over the country for it ; but were unsuccessful in procuring a copy ; the only one then known was in the British Museum, a transcript of which is printed entire in the first volume of the above work."—Heawood's *Coronation at Manchester*, p. 7, note.

Another copy of this sermon is in the collection of James Crossley, Esq., F.S.A., the President of the Chetham Society.

John Dunton, in his *Life and Errors*, gives a list of provincial booksellers, and amongst them is—

"Mr. Clayton in Manchester. He was apprentice to Mr. Johnson of the same town; but, his master thinking it necessary to be a knave, and as a consequence to walk off, Mr. Clayton succeeds him, and has stepped into the whole business of that place, which is very considerable; and, if he have but prudence, he may thrive apace."

From Mr. Hotten's *Handbook to the Topography of England and Wales* I extract the following :—

"2546. Manchester Bookseller in 1697. Gipps (Thos., Rector of Bury) Against corrupting the Word of God, Preacht at Christ Church in Manchester upon a publick Occasion. 4to . . . Manchester: Ephraim Johnston, Bookseller, 1697. . . .*

"2547. Manchester Bookseller in 1698. 'Remarks on Remarks; or the Rector of Bury's Sermon Vindicated; his Charge against the Dissenters for Corrupting the Word of God justified and confirmed, by Thos. Gipps, Rector of Bury, Lancashire. Also the Absurdities and Notorious Falsities of Mr. Owen [of Manchester] Detected.' 4to, pp. 64 . . . Manchester: Ephraim Johnston, Bookseller, 1698.*

"2548.—Ib. 'Tentamen Novum Continuatum, or an Answer to Mr. Owen's Plea and Defence, wherein Bishop Pearson's Chronology about the time of St. Paul's Constituting Timothy Bishop of Ephesus, and Titus of Crete, is confirmed, and all Mr. Owen's Arguments drawn from Antiquity overthrown. By Thomas Gipps, Rector of Bury, in Lancashire.' 4to. Manchester: Ephraim Johnston, Bookseller, 1699."*

Johnston was not the only bookseller in Manchester at this date :—

"Tutamen Evangelicum; or, a Defence of Scripture Ordination, against the Exceptions of T[homas] G[ipps]. In a Book intituled Tentamen Novum, proving that

---

* In the Library of James Crossley, Esq., F.S.A. These pamphlets are also described in Fishwick's *Lancashire Library*, p. 392.

Ordination by Presbyters is Valid; Timothy and Titus were no Diocesan Rulers; The Presbyters of Ephesus were the Apostles' Successors in the Government of that Church, and not Timothy; The First Epistle to Timothy was Written before the Meeting at Miletus; The Ancient Waldenses had no Diocesan Bishops, &c. &c. By the Author of the Plea for Scripture Ordination [James Owen] . . . London: Printed for Zachary Whitworth, Bookseller in Manchester, 1697."*

I again quote from Mr. Hotten's *Handbook :—*

"2570. Old Manchester Broadsides. Two most curious rudely engraved sheets for Children, containing figures of Adam and Eve, Mare-maid, Parrot, a Lap Dog, Unicorn, the Brown Cow gives best Milk, a fatt tame Bear, a large Camell, Galloping Bob, a Oule, a fine stout [*sic*] Horse, &c., &c., with old Manchester Cries, Buy my Ink, Onions, Oysters, Rediches, Laces, &c., in all 51 curious little pictures, designed in the drollest possible style, probably unique, £3. 15s. Sold at the Toy Shop over against the Angel, near the Cross, in Manchester (1700).

"A very curious little picture of St. Ann's Church is given, also the portraits of William III. and Mary. The date, therefore, will probably be about 1698-1710.

"2544. . . . Wroe (Dr. R., Warden of Christ's College in Manchester), Discourse in the Collegiate Church of Manchester on the Day of Her Majesty's happy Accession to the Throne. 4to. . . . Published at the Request of the Town, 1704."*

This, like the preceding works named, was probably printed in London. In January, 1719, commenced the *Manchester Weekly Journal*, printed by Roger Adams, *price one penny.* "No. 325, dated March 15, 1725, was in the possession of the late Mr. John Yates of Bolton; and in the imprint it states as printed in 'Smiby-door'" [*i.e.* Smithy-door]. (Timperley, *Dictionary of Printers*, p. 621.)

In a foot-note Mr. Timperley adds, "During Mr. Yates's residence at Chesterfield I often saw this paper, but am sorry to say it is now destroyed."

---

* In Fishwick's Lanc. Lib. p. 419 the imprint is given as follows: "London, printed by J. H. for Henry Morflock." This and several other sermons by Warden Wroe are in the Chetham Library.

To Roger Adams, we believe, is due the honour of having printed the first book in Manchester :—

"Mathematical Lectures; being the first and second that were read to the Mathematical Society at Manchester. By the late ingenious Mathematician John Jackson. 'Who can number the sands of the Sea, the drops of Rain, and the Days of Eternity?'—Eccles. i. 2. 'He that telleth the number of the Stars, and calleth them all by their Names.'—Psalm cxlvii. 4. Manchester: Printed by Roger Adams, in the Parsonage, and sold by William Clayton, Bookseller, at the Conduit, 1719."

A copy of this rare and curious work is in the library of James Crossley, Esq., F.S.A., who gave some account of its author in an early volume of "N. & Q." (1st S. iv. 300).

There was a bookseller in Manchester named Thomas Hodges, who *published* a Charge of Bishop Peploe.

Manchester typography about this time seems to have been closely allied with science. Thus we learn from Mr. Hotten that in 1732 R. Whitworth printed Gamaliel Smethurst's *Tables of Time*,*† and soon after appeared a little book which had not met the eye of Mr. De Morgan when he published his *Arithmetical Books*. It may be well on this account to transcribe the title-page :—

"The Merchant's Companion, and Tradesman's Vade Mecum: or Practical Arithmetick, both Vulgar and Decimal, Rendered more clear, short, and easy, than ever before. In which Most of the Rules of Arithmetic are altered to Advantage, and New Methods laid down, whereby the young Scholar may, with Ease, become a Proficient in a Short Time. Together with An Appendix For those who are advanced in Accompts, Containing Mensuration, both superficial and Solid; as also many

---

* In the Library of James Crossley, Esq., F.S.A.; and another copy in the Manchester Free Library.

† In the Manchester Free Library, and a copy also in the Library of Thomas Baker, Esq., of Skerton House, Old Trafford. Mr. Baker also possesses two numbers of the

Contractions, tho' none that are meerly curious, but such as may be serviceable applied to Trade and Merchandise. The Whole necessary for all men of Business, Teachers of Accompts and their Scholars. By John Saxton, Writing Master and Accomptant in Manchester. Manchester: Printed by R. Whitworth; and sold by the Author and the Booksellers in Manchester, and by C. Rivington at the Bible and Crown in St. Paul's Church Yard, London. Price 2s. 6d. 1737." * †

No earlier examplar of our Manchester press than that already named appears to be known, and yet it seems probable that some may hereafter be found. Mr. John Owen of Manchester has favoured me with the following, which he copied from an entry in the registers of the Manchester Cathedral :—

"1693. March.—Jonathan, son of John Green, Manchester, Printer, baptised."

It is also possible that some of the Lancashire Civil War Tracts, issued *s.l.*, may have been the fruits of a local press. Since the first appearance of this note it has been stated that a book entitled " A Guide to Heaven," was printed at Smithy Door in 1664.

The authority is an entry in one of Ford's catalogues. (See papers by Mr. J. P. Earwaker, F.S.A., and Mr. W. H. Allnutt in Local Gleanings, relating to Lancashire and Cheshire, vol. i., p. 55.)

Lancashire Journal, printed by John Berry at the Dial near the Cross, Manchester. They are Nos. 57 and 61, July 30, and Aug. 27, 1739. (See Harland's ed. of Baines, i. 329.) These are the earliest relics known to be in existence of Manchester newspaper literature. To the courtesy of Mr. Baker and Mr. Crossley the writer has been much indebted in drawing up this notice.

HUMPHREY CHETHAM'S CHURCH LIBRARIES.

[The following account of these foundations was contributed by the present writer to *Country Words*, 1867]:—

We of Manchester are proud and justly so of the name of Humphrey Chetham, and when we see one of those quaintly dressed youths who appear to have walked out of some picture painted by Lely or Dobson, when the merry monarch reigned in England, we may think with love of the gentle spirit which held out for all time a helping hand to those who need it most, which essayed to comfort the widow and to wipe away the tears of the fatherless.

Sitting in the reading-room of the Chetham Library, surrounded by its treasures of literature, we have often been struck, when looking at the founder's portrait, with the earnest melancholy look of his face, marked with deep lines of thought and care. It is plain that he was no light-hearted mortal who could make a jest of everything beneath the sun, but a man to whom life was a sad and solemn reality ; a man who had fought hardly in the great battle, and who carried on him many marks of conflict. So little is known of the personal history and tastes of this old Manchester worthy that anything casting, however faint, a light upon them must be welcome. And amongst his minor charities, there is one that has about it something so characteristic alike of the man and of his times and is withal so little known, that we purpose in this paper to give a brief account of it.

His will contains the following paragraph :—" Also, I do hereby give and bequeath the sum of two hundred pounds to be bestowed by my executors in Godly English books, such as Calvin's, Preston's, and Perkins's works ; comments and annotations of the Bible or some parts thereof ; or such other books as the said Richard

Johnson, John Tildesley, and Mr. Hollingworth, or any of them shall think most proper for the edification of the common people; to be by discretion of my said executors chained upon desks, or to be fixed to the pillars, or in any convénient places in the parish churches of Manchester and Boulton-in-the-Moors, and in the chapels of Turton, Walmsley, and Gorton, in the said county of Lancaster, within one year next after my decease."

Some years elapsed before the books were placed in the Collegiate Church of Manchester; and the delay seems to have chafed the spirit of good Henry Newcome, in whose diary there are several entries relative to the English Library, as he styles Chetham's bequest. To Newcome fell the task of setting them up in the Jesus chantry of the Byrom chapel.*

These books have now disappeared; the last remnants of them were disposed of some years ago by the authorities to a bookseller in Shudehill, from whose possession they passed into the collection of James Crossley, Esq., F.S.A. The libraries of Bolton and Walmsley have also vanished, but those of Gorton and Turton still remain.

At Gorton there are fifty-six volumes chained to an iron rod, running midway between the top and bottom of a dark oaken book case, surmounted by a carved inscription—THE GIFT OF HVMPHREY CHETHAM ESQVIRE 1655. The Turton bookcase is of a similar character, and contains fifty-two volumes; but the rod on which the chains traversed had been lost, and the chains wrapped round the volumes to which they belonged, to the great detriment of the binding. It is needless to say that the wear and tear of two centuries had considerably deteriorated the condition of the books, and that some of them had become very imperfect, having in a manner been read away.

In 1855, however, these libraries attracted the notice

---

* Newcome's Diary, pp. 12, 30, 127, &c.

of Mr. G. J. French, and by his exertions subscriptions were obtained for the purpose of restoring them to their original condition, which has accordingly been done, and the books are now as available for the subjects of Queen Victoria as they were for the lieges of the Lord Protector in the year of their commencement, 1655.*

We learn from Fuller that the books comprising these collections were such as their founder himself delighted in; but it is a matter of doubt whether they will be as much read now as they were by Humphrey Chetham more than two hundred years ago. Modern piety is content with meagre fare, and would probably hesitate to attack a ponderous folio of seven hundred or a thousand pages, and it is books of this nature which fill the shelves of Chetham's Church Libraries.

The piety and learning of Jewel and Ussher have scarcely preserved them from entire neglect; Burroughs, Gouge, and Greenham are rarely heard of now; and few but the bookworm care for Mede's "Diatribæ," or Peter Martyr's "Commonplaces."

The "Acts and Monuments of the Christian Church," by John Foxe ("The Book of Martyrs") is as popular now as when it first issued from the press of John Day: long may it continue so, not to foster any spirit of sectarian partizanship, but to show an age somewhat deficient in earnestness how nobly and grandly the men of old could suffer and die in the defence of truth. Another book amongst those which has retained its hold upon the national mind is Baxter's "Saints' Rest," which was a new book just rising into popularity when it was purchased by Chetham's executors. They appear to have selected in a somewhat liberal spirit, the various shades of Protestant opinion being fairly represented, and the collection forms an interesting memento of the religious literature of that age, which, above all others in English

---

* Bibliographical Account.   See note, next page.

history, was most strongly marked by the influences of theology. You can fancy one of Cromwell's Ironsides reading, with grim piety, "Calvin on Job," or Beard's "Theatre of God's Judgments."

Some of these volumes have a special interest for the antiquary of Lancashire, notably the works of Robert Bolton, of Blackburn; Isaac Ambrose's "Prima, Media, and Ultima;" and the works of John White, the learned Vicar of Eccles. In the preface to the "Way to the True Church," by the last-named, we find the follow curious bit of Lancashire folk-lore, which he has labelled in the margin, "The manner how the vulgar sort of people . . . say their prayers . .

THE LITTLE CREED.
Little creed can I need,
Kneele before our Ladies knee;
Candles light, candles burne,
Our Ladie prayed to her deare Sonne
That we might all to heaven come.
Little creed. Amen.

"This that followeth they call the White Paternoster :—

White Paternoster, Saint Peter's brother,
What hast i' t' one hand ? White boak leaves
What hast i' t' other hand ? Heauven yate keyes.
Open heauven yates, and steike hell yates,
And let every crysome childe creep to it owne mother.
White Paternoster. Amen.

"Another prayer :—

I blesse me with God and the rood,
With his sweet flesh and precious blood,
With his crosse and his creed,
With his length and his breed,
From my toe to my crowne,
And all my body up and downe,
From my backe to my breast,
My five wits be my rest,
God, let never ill come at ill
But through Jesus own will.
Sweet Jesus Lord. Amen.

"Many also vse to weare Vervein against blasts: and

when they gather it for this purpose, first they crosse the herbe with their hand, and then they bless it, thus :—

Hallowed be thou Vervein as thou growest on the ground,
For in the mount of Calvary there thou was first found,
Thou healedst our Saviour Jesus Christ, and stanchedst
    his bleeding wound ;
In the name of the Father, the Sonne, and the Holy
    Ghost, I take thee from the ground."*

"Quaint pickings," it has been said, "fall to the readers of curious books;" and those who read merely for amusement and without any higher aim, may find in some of these antique tomes ample food for the mos voracious appetite.

Perhaps no book in the language contains more varied and out of the way knowledge than Dr. George Hakewill's "Apologie." "Wherever," says Mr. French, "this goodly and corpulent folio is opened, there is always something to arrest the attention." Acting on this hint we open the book at random, and our eye rests upon this passage : "I confess I have often wondered not a little at Seneca's bold prophetical spirit touching that discovery [of America]—

    In later times an age shall rise
    Wherein the ocean shall the bands
    Of things enlarge : there shall likewise
    New worlds appear, and mighty lands
    Typhis discover, then Thule
    The world's end shall no longer be."†

But these books have had a higher and nobler office to fulfil than merely amusing. For the last two hundred years they have yielded comfort and solace to weary spirits and reproof to erring souls. Who shall estimate the extent of their influence, or chronicle the lives to which they may have given stability and purpose ?

Perhaps, in some measure, we may now consider them superseded; but they must ever be looked upon with veneration and respect, as a relic of one whose memory is loved by all who know the story of his life.

---

* Bibliographical Account, p. 52.　　† Hakewill, p. 249.

THE BOOK RARITIES OF THE MAN-CHESTER FREE LIBRARY.

[Reprinted from the Transactions of the Manchester Literary Club. Volume 1.

A special meeting of the Manchester Literary Club was held on Tueday evening, February 23, 1875, in the large hall of the Free Reference Library in Campfield, to examine a portion of the rare books in the collection and to hear an address concerning them from Mr W. E' A. Axon. There was a large attendance, including several ladies The Free Libraries Committee had kindly placed the room and volumes at the disposal of the members of the Club for this evening, opportunity having been taken of an occasion when the Reference Department is temporarily closed for revision and re-arrangement A large selection of books had been carefully classified and arranged on tables extending the length of the room, and more than an hour was spent in inspecting the volumes At eight o'clock the chair was taken by the President (Mr. J H Nodal), and Mr. Axon proceeded to describe the history and chief characteristics of the books on the tables before him in an extempore address, the substance of which is given in the following pages. At the close,

The PRESIDENT said they were greatly indebted to Mr Axon for his extremely interesting address It would convey to the minds of most of those present, as it did to his, an idea of the riches of the Free Library, of which previously they had but a very slight and wholly inadequate conception One reason for this ignorance was undoubtedly the unfortunate location of the building The varied and valuable stores accumulated by the town during the twenty-one years' existence of the Library, were virtually valueless to the majority of the literary and professional men of the city, the journalists, lawyers, and people of studious tastes solely on account of the out-of-the-way, inconvenient situation of the Library. He trusted that before long the Reference Department at any rate would be removed to a more central and convenient site, and unquestionably the value of the institution would thereby be enormously increased.

Mr. CHARLES HARDWICK moved, and Mr. J. HIGSON HAWORTH seconded, a hearty vote of thanks to the chairman and members of the Free Libraries Committee for placing the Library at the service of the Club, and to Dr. Crestadoro, Mr. Sutton, and the assistant librarians for their courtesy and attention. Both speakers testified in terms of high praise to the uniform kindness of the Library officials to all who had occasion to consult the collection. The resolution was carried unanimously, and the examination of the volumes on the tables was then resumed.]

[The figures inserted in brackets are the numbers of the volumes in the Catalogue of the Free Reference Library, and are inserted for the convenience of those who may wish to consult them.]

The rarity of books is one of the mysteries of the librarian's profession. To outsiders it must sometimes seem strange that one book should possess a pecuniary value enormously disproportionate to that of others which, for all practical purposes, might seem to be of equal value and utility. No doubt there are many who, in this age of shilling Shaksperes and penny Bunyans, will be surprised to hear of £800 being paid for a single copy of Shakespere. It is not until a certain acquaintance has been made with books and literary history that we come to see the reason of this great difference. To a company like the present, who are all either literary or at least have literary tastes, there is no need of explaining the causes, but it may not be out of place to indicate some of the varieties which exist in what may be called the rarities and curiosities of books.

There are rare books and rare books It is possible to class them in something like order, or at least to arrange them in groups   Some of these varieties will be named, and then attention will be drawn to certain series of books which have been placed upon the tables to illustrate certain phases of literary history. As a preliminary, however, it should be observed that for the most part the books named are to be taken only as samples of the class to which they belong. The exhibition is not intended to bo one exhaustive of the rare and curious books in the collection. Indeed the two departments in which the Manchester Free Library is probably strongest—English History and Political Economy — have scarcely been laid under contribution at all. The library contains some four thousand volumes of tracts relating to Political Economy and to the history of trade and commerce   These contain many valuable illustrations of the social and political changes of the past, and are well worth a special treatment On the present occasion the chief object is to show the very diverse riches of the library, and the widely-separated studies which it can aid.

Of some books so few copies are printed that when these few have been subjected to the wear and tear, and the accidents of time and fortune of half a century, their seldom recurrence in the market is no matter for wonder   On the table is "Bibliographiania" [2076], a work by a band of Manchester book-lovers. Only twenty-four copies were printed of it. Hence it was rare from the day it first saw the light   There is a translation of a portion of the satires of Horace into Italian [28803], very rare and interesting on many accounts   It was printed at the expense of an English lady, who took a deep interest in Italian literature. Of it 150 copies were printed, and it was illustrated with some extremely beautiful engravings. The translation was by Cardinal Consalvi, and the printing by the widow of Bodoni. Of Dibdin's Specimen Bibliothecæ Britannicæ [27907] only forty copies were printed. There are some books of which there is no reason to suppose a small number was printed, but of which very few now remain. One of the rarest of rare books is what is called the first London Directory [14305]. This copy is one of the three or four known to be in existence. It is additionally interesting from containing the autograph of Thomas Hearne, the celebrated antiquary. This book may almost be cited as a proof of Darwinism in literature. Place it side by side with its descendant of the present year, and the contrast is indeed amusing.

Certain wealthy lovers of literature have amused their leisure by printing. One of the most famous private printing presses was that of Horace Walpole, Earl of Orford, who printed a number of curious books. On the tables are a number of specimens of the Strawberry Hill press [24918]. Another private printing press was the property of Sir Egerton Brydges [3131], where some very beautiful specimens were turned out, some of which are exhibited. Then there are books not printed for sale. The Dante, edited by Lord Vernon [32456], is a magnificent example of a book, printed for presentation to scholars and others. Another of great interest is the edition of Sir John Fortescue's works, collected by his descendant Lord Claremont [31674].

Another class of rare literary productions is composed of books written by English or other authors in their vernacular tongue, but printed abroad. Some few English authors had a taste that way, and several works of Sir Egerton Brydges were printed at Geneva [3139, 32103-4]. Sometimes, however, this arose from compulsory circumstances, as in the case of exiles for religious or political causes. A number of examples will be found; amongst them is one of the earliest translations of the New Testament into English. It was printed at Antwerp about 1539, for the religious refugees [23345]. The Florence Miscellany [18342] was printed at that city by a number of English friends belonging to the Della Cruscan school of literature. The very curious works, privately printed at Paris by Francis Egerton, Earl of Bridgewater, should also be named [1731-2].

Many books, and some of them very important ones, have been rigidly suppressed by the Governments of the different countries in which they were printed Let me call your attention to one of the Marprelate tracts [30714] so intimately connected with the history of Puritanism and dissent. This was Penry's reply to a sermon preached by Dr Bancroft, attacking the English Nonconformists Many books have also been suppressed by their authors. An example is the Shadows of the Clouds, by Zeta [21254]. It was really written by Mr. Froude, the historian, who is said to have afterwards recalled every possible copy. The Barrow's Remains [1467], as edited by Dr. Lee, the first Bishop of Manchester, is another notable example

Some books are rare in certain forms There is a copy of Sharp's Coventry Mysteries [26984] and in that form only seventy-five copies were printed. Then there are books in little known languages. The Library is rich in that class. It possesses a collection of Bibles, or portions of Bibles, in about 140 different languages, and as there are perhaps not more than twelve civilized tongues, it is evident that many are in languages very little known. One curious example of a book printed in a little-known language is a tract in the Mongolian tongue [37421]. The author was a Scotchman, Mr R. Yuille. In his MS. account of the book and himself the author said that he made the press and the matrices and cast two founts of type, one in the Mongolian and the other in the Thibetan tongue. His Mongolian pupils were the only help he had, and they "all became expert young men both at type-making and printing, and also in their classical education."

Some books are distinguished by curious verbal errors or peculiarities, *e.g.*, the "Breeches" Bible [2026]. Walton's Polyglot Bible [24961] is found in two states. Originally issued during the Commonwealth, it was dedicated to Cromwell, but the winds of State blowing back Charles II. to the throne, the "Republican" leaf was cancelled, and another dedicated to that religious king inserted instead. Books are sometimes curious from being printed in an unusual fashion. Macray's Golden Lyre [28115], a collection of English and foreign poems, is printed in golden letters. A still more remarkable production is the fac-simile of Magna Charta [36247], printed in burnished gold, and illustrated in water colours by Whittaker, who invented the process by which it was printed.

Another class consists of historical productions, in which the authors have sought to put everything topsy-turvy. Such is the attempt by Horace Walpole [24921] to show that Richard III. is a very much misunderstood individual, and another [33871] in which O'Brien tried to prove that Robespierre was an extremely amiable party. Some books are interesting as showing anticipations of modern inventions, or early notices of modern industries. Thus Porta [18788] is said to have anticipated Pepper's Ghost, and Lana's Prodromo [33379] contains the first scheme (like most of its successors— impracticable) for aerial navigation.

Early editions of famous books are always curious, and sometimes have a special literary value of their own. There are on the table early editions of the productions of English writers, such as Drayton [28441-2], Ben Jonson [12786], Spenser [22258], Chaucer [4534], and Pope [28040]. There is also a first edition of Milton's Paradise Lost [15961], which was then published in ten books, the first edition of Selden's Table Talk [21166], and the first edition of Vathek [1674]. Let me draw especial attention to the first edition of Hume's Essays

[11870], containing very curious deviations from the later copies   Amongst the Shakspeiiana exhibited is the second folio [21266] and the fourth folio [21267], which contains the seven spurious plays   The most cuiious Shaksperean relic here is a book of fac-similes of his Shaksperean forgeries [34316] by the great forger, William Henry Ireland   They were executed by him to show his ability to imitate old writings, which had been doubted

Other books are rendered valuable by the autographs in them   Here is a volume—Montagu's Acts and Monuments [16189]—which acquires interest from the circumstance that it formerly belonged to the author of the Anatomy of Melancholy, who has written his name in it.   Many books in the collection have in them the autograph of Southey [12610]   Delambre's Histoire de l'Astronomie contains the autographs of Delambre and Arago   Another book before me is especially interesting, as it at one time belonged to David Garrick, and has in it his book-plate [24902].   The motto which Garrick selected is one worthy to be written in gold   "La première chose qu'on doit faire quand on a emprunté un livre, c'est de le lire afin de pouvoir le rendre plûtot" Menagiana, vol. iv.   There is another volume which has been in the possession of Sir James Macintosh, and a Shakspeie [21266] which was once the property of a famous Lancashire man, John Philip Kemble

Of manuscripts the library possesses but few   Perhaps the most curious is the autobiography of William Stout, the Lancashiie Quaker [22643].   It was published by the late John Harland, and the manuscript then pre_ sented to the library foi due preservation.   There is also a spiritual autobiography of Sir James Fraser of Brae [9352]; an orthographical MS , dated 1474 [29979]; Harland's collections for a History of Shorthand [32982]; a number of old deeds relating to the district, amongst them an early copy of the Great Charter of Manchester, and some others.

Having thus named some of the various classes of rare and curious books, it now remains to point to one or two special groups. A number of local books are exhibited, amongst them the sermon preached at the death of Humphrey Chetham (nephew of the founder), by Livesey [14176]; John Howard's book on Prisons, printed and written at Warrington [11730]; a book printed at Blackley in 1791 [11754]; an early edition of Tim Bobbin [28257]; the Gleaner, an old Manchester periodical; the first edition of Bamford's poems [1178]; the "Festive Wreath" [26640], being the contributions of a number of literary friends who met at what was called the Poet's Corner in Old Millgate, read pieces at their meetings, and had them printed in what is now a volume of rare occurrence; Clarke's School Candidates; an early work by Harrison Ainsworth [302]; Outward Bound, a privately printed poem by Mr. Hugh Birley, M.P. [31705]; and Within and Without, an early work by Dr. George M'Donald, presented to the Manchester Free Library "in grateful acknowledgment of literary aid" afforded to the author [14697]. The library possesses a large number of books and pamphlets illustrative of the history of the district. It carefully preserves reports and the ephemeral papers which in a few years will be vainly sought elsewhere.

There are a number of herbal and other books, so arranged as to show the history of the art of representing flowers and plants. The old herbals are still charming books to read. The word-painting in old Gerard is often of a very finished character. We have here Matthiolus 1571 [28088]; Dodoen's Niewe Herball, Lond., 1578 [28036]; Gerard's Herball, Lond., 1636 [28071]; Parkinson's Theater of Plants, 1640 [17583]; Chabræus, Stirpium Icones, 1666 [30359]; Aldrovandus, 1668 [34896]; Ray, Hist. Plant.,

1693 [29464]; Tournefort's Herbal, 1719 [23842]; Curtis's Flora Londinensis, 1777-1828 [6223]; Plenok, Icones Plant. Med., 1788 [34013]; Bolton's Halifax Funguses, 1788-91 [2364]; Sowerby's English Botany, 1790-1843 [22146]; Macdonald's Gardener's Dictionary, 1807 [14694]; Roscoe's Monandrian Plants, 1828 [34198]; Blume, Flora Javæ, 1828 [27199]; Wallich, Plantæ Asiaticæ Rariores, 1831 [29603]; Warner's Orchids, 1862-5 [27626]; Blume, Orchidées, 1864 [27213]. Along with these have been placed an herbarium, containing plants gathered and mounted by the great chemist Dalton [6303], and a collection of mosses made by the gentle-hearted Richard Buxton, an artizan naturalist of great power, whose life was passed in grimy Ancoats.

A series of books have been arranged on the tables to illustrate the history of printing and of book illustration from the infancy of printing to the present time. First will be found about one hundred volumes, which issued from the press between the years 1477 and 1600. Amongst *incunabula* " cradle-books " are some very fine specimens of printing. It may be doubted whether the paper and ink of the present day will preserve their texture and brilliance so successfully. All books printed before 1600 have a certain degree of rarity. It will be sufficient, however, to name those on the tables which issued from the press prior to 1520.

Bible en Duytsche   Delf. 1477   [2023]
Carchani Sermones. Basiliæ 1479   [35227]
Vallensis de Lingua Latini. Venet. 1480   [37217.]
Biblia. " Fontibus ex Græcis, &c." 1481   [35034]
Statuta Provincialia Dioecesis Constantiensis   Spiræ.
   1482. [29996]
The Golden Legend. 2nd edit Caxton 1483. [28512]
Manipulus Curatorum a Guidone de Monte Rochen.
   1484 [10185.]
Platinæ Vitæ Pontificum. 1485. [18417.]
Rolewinck, Fasciculus Temporoum. Argent. 1488
   [28808]
Seneca, Omnia Opera. Venet. 1492. [28780.]

Passionael unde dat Levend der Hylghen. 1492. [28778.]
Augustini Liber Epistolarum. Basil. 1493. [34941.]
Caoursini Descriptio Obsidionis Rhodiæ. Ulmæ Reger.
    1496. [3813.]
Plinii Junioris Epistola. Venet. 1501. [29980.]
Boetius de Philosophico Consolatu. Argent. 1501.
    [2331.]
Aristotelis de Celo et Mundo [and other works].   Lypt-
    zigk. 1504-7. [29015-19.]
Valerij Maximi. Liptz. 1506. [29022.]
Aristotelis Excerpta. Liptz. 1506. [28777.]
Mantuani Bucolica. Argent. 1507. [29981.]
Ciceronis Epistolæ Familiares. Lyptzigk. 1507. [29022.]
Cicero de Amicitia. Lyptzigk. 1507. [20021.]
Scripta : seu Expositiones Antonii Andree. Venet. 1509.
    [28806.]
Statuta Ordinis Cartusiensis a Domno Guigone. Basil.
    1510. [10186.]
Augustin sur le Psaultier. Paris. 1511. [28810.]
Eusebii Cæsariensis Episcopi Chronicon. Paris. 1512.
    [8116.]
Damianus de Expeditione in Turcas Elegeia, &c. Basil.
    Froben. 1515. [29982.]
Catonis Præcepta Moralia, &c. Argent. 1516. [29983.]
Hutten, Nemo. Aug. Vindel. 1518. [29984.]
Eusebii Ecclesiastica Historia. Argent. 1518. [8117.]

The most interesting of these, to us at least, is the
Golden Legend, from the press of the first English
printer. This book of Voragine's is a most wonderful
collection of tales concerning the saints, the narrative
including not only what they did in their lives, but in
some cases what they did after their deaths. The lives
are illustrated by woodcuts, which in size and form
remind one of the *cartes* of the present day. There is a
vigour and decision of outline about them unknown to
modern art. There is no complete copy of Caxton's
Golden Legend known, as the Life of St. Thomas of
Canterbury is usually wanting in copies otherwise
approaching completeness. This copy is a mere frag-
ment, and yet a precious relic of the far-seeing mercer
to whom England owes the art of printing. The long
array of books upon the tables will show how impossible ·

it is that I should call attention to the specialities of each·
A very rapid naming of a few of them must suffice.
Here is the first edition of Foxe's Book of Martyrs
[28063], and also the second edition [38076]. At one
time this was, next to the Bible, the best read book
in the country. A fine folio of Chaucer, 1561
[4534]. Stowe's Annals [28281, 28076]. The famous
Bible of Ferrara, printed in that city in 1553 for
the benefit of the Jews [2068]. Luciani Dialogi, with
"the Aldine anchor on its opening page" [14477]. Specimens of other famous presses are also exhibited, *e.g.*,
books printed by Plantin [14095], Baskerville [28805,
34969], and Bodoni [9910]. It is interesting to trace, by
the aid of these books, the progress of pictorial art as
applied to literature. The rude woodcuts of Caxton
[28512] and Reger [3813] were succeeded by the artistic
vigour and excellence which marks the illustrations to
Foxe. Only a few years before Foxe appeared Lycos-
thenis Prodigiorum Chronicon, Basil, 1557 [33501], the
woodcuts in which are vigorous though utterly destitute
of artistic merit. The book is well worth examination,
and contains a sufficient number of "Siamese Twins"
to set up every fair in the United Kingdom. The
degradation of wood engraving in the early part of the
eighteenth century should be contrasted with the beauty
of some of the illustrations to Aldrovandus in the latter
part of the seventeenth century. The tradition of the wood
engraver's art seems to have been lost for a time, and it
has been said that a Manchester printer—Imison—was
one of the first to recover it. A book from his press
[30269] has pictures in it coarse enough to have been
executed with a butcher's cleaver. The development of
the modern art of wood engraving by the genius of
Bewick [2000-3] and his pupils has been the means of
diffusing a love and knowledge of the most beautiful
forms of art in the humblest homes. On the tables will
be found fine modern specimens of book-illustration,

the steel engravings of the Turner Gallery [34624], the
lithographs of the Galerie d'Orleans [36375]; the
chromo-lithographs of the specimens from the Art
Treasures Exhibition [30156-61]; the etchings in the
Portfolio and in Hamerton's Etchings and Etchers
[32959]; and finally the magnificent photographs of
Bradford's Arctic Regions [35123].   This is a speical
feature of the exhibition to which I wish to call attention, for this series is really an epitome of the history of
the printing press considered as the interpreter alike of
Author and of Artist.

BELLOT COLLECTION OF CHINESE BOOKS.

The Public Library of the city of Manchester possesses a small collection of Chinese books, which it owes to the liberality of the late Thomas Bellot, Esq., M.R.C.S. The bequeather was a man of considerable philological attainments. His little work on Sanskrit derivations of English words, now a rare book, fetches a high price when it comes into the market. He was a friend of Bopp the translator of the Aphorisms of Hippokrates, and the first (and perhaps the only one) to make English Galen's Treatise on the Hand. Occasionally he contributed an article to the pages of Notes and Queries. In an early volume (1st S. x. 168), of that chatty periodical, there is a communication from him on the subject of the best method of learning the Chinese language. In the eleventh report of the Library we find noticed the " donation of the Bellot collection of Chinese books and ancient Chinese bronzes, bequeathed by the late Thomas Bellot, R.N., to become the property of the Manchester Free Library at the death of his surviving brother, William Henry Bellot, M.D. This gentleman has given up at once a portion of the collection ; the remainder of the books, together with the bronzes, are to be transferred to the Free Library after his death." The portion of the collection already acquired extends to 253 volumes, exclusive of sundry specimens of paper, &c. The collection does not include the Imperial Dictionary of Kang-he, although it has the following dictionaries: the Ching Tsze Tung, the Luh Shoo Tung, the Shwo Wan, the Tsaou Tse Hwuy ; the Tsze luy le yuen. Some of these are much rarer than that issued under the patronage of Kang-he, and are of greater importance to the student of Chinese antiquities. Of works on the fine arts and archæology, we may name Keae tsze yuen shoo, *Book of the Mustard Seed Garden*, Keae tsze yuen shoo hwa, *Paintings and Writings of the Mustard Seed Garden*, Keae tsze yuen hwa chuen, *Description of the Paintings of the Mustard Seed Garden*, Po Koo t' hoo, *Universal Antiquities Illustrated.* This work includes plates of antiquities of the Shang, Chow, and Han dynasties. The first portion is given to the English public in Mr. Thom's "Ancient Chinese Vases." The Yuh too poo, Illustrations of Prehnite, Shih chuh chae shoo hwa poo, on Writing and Drawing; Tseih koo chae, on Ancient Vase Inscriptions; Yin teen, the Canon of Seals; Yuen ting tseen luh, Register of Metal Coins. These works we commend to the editor of the Universal Art Catalogue, since none of them appear in the proof sheets of that useful bibliography; and also the Urh Ya, an encyclopœdic work, in ten folio volumes, and "adorned" with pictures of possible and impossible objects, animate and inanimate. Amongst the Buddhist works are the Hwa Yen King, Lotus of the Good Law, King Kong King Diamond Sutra (which has been translated into English by the Rev. S. Beal), two or three of the rituals of the goddess Kwan yin, and various prayer books in vogue amongst the followers of Gautama. There is also a copy of the surgical drawings, known as the T'hung jin ming thong che t'hoo, Brass Man of the Imperial Audience Chamber. Doctors in the celestial empire are sometimes accused of killing more than they cure. "A physician," says Dr. Dudgeon, "is the only man who can kill another with impunity. . . . . Litigation does, however, take place sometimes, as the result of death from acupuncture. The case is always decided in favour of the doctor, if it can be shown that he has punctured the bloodvessels in the places laid down on the Brass Man (acupuncture figure in the College), or from the recognised diagrams" (Chinese Recorder, March, 1870). There are no poetical works in the collection, and only two novels, one of which, Te sze tsae tse, keae tse yuen, a novel of the fourth order, entitled The Mustard Seed Garden, is embellished with some good specimens of Chinese art. Of the well-known Thousand Character Classic, there are several editions, one accompanied by a Mandchoo translation. It only remains to add that the Library Committee have liberally supplemented the Bellot Library, by the purchase of Morrison's Chinese Dictionary, the grammar by the Rev. J. Summers, and the much more important Syntaxe Nouvelle de la Langue Chinoise of the veteran sinologue, M. Stanislas Julien.—*Trübner's Library Record*, ii. 790, *July* 25, 1870.

PITMAN'S PHONETIC JOURNAL.

The Reference Library at Campfield has just been enriched by a donation from Mr. Isaac Pitman, of Bath, the well-known inventor of Phonography. It consists of a set of the *Phonetic Journal*, extending to thirty volumes, from its commencement in 1842 up to the present time. The first volume is a slender 12mo. of only 96 pages, whilst the last is a royal 8vo. of 436 pages. These volumes contain the entire history of the beautiful art of Phonography, and of Mr. Pitman's attempts to reform English spelling, and they include nearly everything that has been written during thirty years on the science of Phonetics. Although Phonography was not born in Manchester, yet the *Phonetic Journal* was. Mr Isaac Pitman was lecturing and teaching his Phonetic shorthand in this city in 1841, and happening to be in the offices of Messrs. Bradshaw and Blacklock, Mr. John Barnes and Mr. Timothy Walker who were in the office, said to him "We can do something to promote your object in this way. If you will write a page of shorthand on a particular kind of paper, and with a particular kind of ink, which we will supply, we will produce you an exact printed copy of it." Mr. Pitman knew nothing then of lithography but the result of his experiment was the issue of an edition of a thousand copies of No. I. of the *Phonographic Journal* (such was the title first used), from the establishment of Messrs. Bradshaw and Blacklock. The number for June, 1845, is the only one deficient in this set, and it is to be hoped that some Manchester phonographer will supply this want.— *Manchester City News*, Jan. 27, 1872.

THE OLD SUBSCRIPTION LIBRARY.

There is doubt even as to the year when this collection began. Aston avers that it was instituted in 1757, but the official records did not go further back than 1765. The original shares were 10s. each, and the annual subscription 6s., but the payments gradually advanced in amount, until the entrance fee was ten guineas and the annual subscription one guinea. Amongst the early subscribers were Messrs. Edward Byrom, Rev. Dr. Griffith, Charles White, F.R.S., Richard Towneley, T. B. Bayley, and Dr. Percival. The prices paid for 622 vols. in 1769 was £287. 19s. 11d. Amongst these was a Chaucer (Thynne's edition, 1532), which cost 2s. 6d.! On the other hand, " Clarissa Harlowe," then in the full zenith of her fame, cost 17s. 6d. The number of volumes at the close of the library's existence would be about 30,000. There were several catalogues issued.

> A Classed Catalogue of the books in the Manchester Subscription Library, Exchange Buildings. Instituted 1765. Manchester: printed by John Harrison, Market-street, 1846. 8vo.

There were numerous supplements to this carefully compiled list. A notice, from which the above data has been chiefly taken, appeared in the *Manchester Guardian*, March 6, 1844. Owing to the then impending demolition of Newall's Buildings, and the inability of the committee to find suitable accommodation elsewhere, the library was sold by public auction in March, 1867.

BISHOP LEE'S LIBRARY.

The terms in which the late Bishop of Manchester bequeathed his library to Owens College, reserved to his wife liberty to select a certain number of volumes from the collection. These volumes came to the hammer at Birmingham, September 14th and 15th, 1875, in consequence of the death of Mrs. Lee. The books fetched high prices. The gem of the sale was a copy of the famous Polyglot Bible, printed at the expense of Cardinal Ximenes. "The Complutensian Polyglot" is the first that was issued, and for critical purposes is less useful than its successors, but as the edition was limited to 600 copies it has always been sought after to a certain extent by bibliomaniacs. At the La Valliere sale, a copy bound in the same style as the Bishop's, sold for £30, and at Willett's sale a copy realised £63. The Bishop's copy was knocked down for £340. A set of Sir W. Dugdale's works reached 245 guineas; "Justiniani Pandectarum' (MS. on vellum), £100. Many of the topographical books sold high; Collinson's Somersetshire, £7. 17s. 6d.; Manning and Bray's Surrey, £18. 10s.; Jones's Brecknockshire, £8. 8s.; Whitaker's Leeds, £13. 2s. 6d.; Shaw's Staffordshire, £42. Roger's collection of prints, 2 vols., large paper, brought six guineas; and the "Vetusta Monumenta," £14. 10s.; the "Florence Gallery" sixteen guineas; and Britton's Cathedrals, £23. A fine subscription copy of Roberts's "Holy Land," with coloured plates, was knocked down at £50. The Polyglot and some other of the rarer books bought by the Rev. Canon Evans, son-in-law of the late Bishop, have since been presented by that gentleman to the Owens College, once more to stand side by side with their ancient companions.

LITERATURE OF THE MANCHESTER ATHENÆUM.

[The following article appeared in the *Manchester Guardian*, Oct. 27th, 1875]:—

The appearance during the present month of the *Manchester Athenæum Gazette* reminds us of some now little known *brochures* that many years ago linked the Athenæum with literature. We are not speaking of the lectures that thirty years ago were so important a feature of the institution, nor are we about to enumerate the brilliant addresses delivered at the *soirées* held from 1843 to 1848, when Dickens, Disraeli, Talfourd, Alison, Emerson, and other famous men electrified their Manchester audiences. The more prominent of these orations have recently been collected in a small volume, and may serve to remind the younger generation of a time when public speaking was cultivated more as an art than it is in the present day. Perhaps the most remarkable of these addresses as an oratorical effort, was that of the Hon. George Sydney Smythe, afterwards Lord Strangford, whose long-sustained flight of eloquence roused his audience to an extraordinary pitch of enthusiasm, the entire meeting rising to their feet at the conclusion and cheering to the very echo.

The *Athenæum Gazette* is the second periodical of its name, and does not differ very materially from its predecessor of a quarter of a century ago, except that the newcomer is twice the size of the old one. In another department of periodical literature we may place the catalogues of the Athenæum library, for with a rapidly increasing collection of books devoted to popular uses the register of its riches cannot be expected to have that permanent character which would be possible for the book list of a library of monastic folios. The library has been several times catalogued. In 1847 appeared an alphabetical catalogue, prepared by Mr. Francis

Espinasse, and which is one of the most satisfactory of its kind ever made of a modern library. The last catalogue is to a certain extent a literary curiosity. It was prepared by the present energetic librarian, and the printed volume was produced at a meeting of the Directors, held on the evening after the destruction of the library by fire. Mr. Dutton is now preparing a catalogue of the library in its present revised and expurgated condition, and the arrangement he has adopted combines many of the advantages of the classified and the alphabetical systems, about which librarians are perpetually arguing. It would lead us too far a-field to discuss the quantity and quality of the contributions to literature that have been made by members of the Athenæum; but the names of Richard Cobden, Sir William Fairbairn, James Crossley, F.S.A.; Charles Swain, James Heywood, F.R.S.; and Francis Espinasse (and the list might be greatly extended) will serve to show that amongst its members have been those who have done service to the State in literature, science, and art.

In 1843 a bazaar was held at the Town Hall in aid of the funds of the institution. One of the objects for sale was a little volume of 51 pages bearing the title of the "Athenæum Souvenir." In this the often-quoted letter of Tom Hood on the delights of literature occupied the post of honour, whilst Swain, "Festus" Bailey, Mary Howitt, Agnes Strickland, Thomas Smelt, Ner Gardiner, George Richardson, Sam Bamford, and other authors, local and strangers, lent a helping hand to the then struggling institution. The book ends with an enigma that claims to be at the head of all enigmas "that ever were penn'd"—

And so great in high places my powers to please,
That a queen lacking me is bereft of all *ease*.

The author would not need to pause for a reply after the italicised revelation.

For this same bazaar was printed a tiny booklet entitled "Stray Leaves; by Iota." These graceful verses were the production of the late Mr. John Harland, F.S.A., whose enthusiasm was not wholly absorbed by the dry-as-dust charms of archæology. Poetic genius he did not possess, but had that sympathetic feeling which may perhaps claim kin with it in a remote degree. His kindly humour found expression also in verse, and he ridicules the "poet's fictions" which form the commonplaces, not perhaps of poets, but certainly of poetasters, and asks—

Who would sigh for his love if her forehead were stone?
Were her eyes real brilliants, who would not groan?
Romantic is he who will hold it a bliss
That from mineral lips he may snatch the cold kiss.

In 1850 there was another bazaar, and in connection with it appeared "The Manchester Athenæum Album, 1850," an elegantly printed quarto volume of 54 pages. Amongst the contributors were Currer Bell, Delta, Charles Swain, Critchley Prince, Dr. John Tyndall, John Stores Smith, Philip James Bailey, Charles Gavan Duffy, &c. Dr. Tyndall's is a charming prose poem, in which the Jungfrau mountain is personified as "a terror to the coward and an inspiration to the brave." Dr. Martin F. Tupper sent some verses written specially for the occasion, the subject being the Manchester Athenæum itself. But certainly the contribution most eagerly scanned would be a brief poem by Alfred Tennyson. As this has not been included in the collected editions of his poems, we may conclude by quoting it in full :—

Here often, when a child, I lay reclined,
   I took delight in this locality.
Here stood the infant Ilion of the mind,
   And here the Grecian ships did seem to be.
And here again I come, and only find
   The drain-cut levels of the marshy lea—
Grey sandbanks, and pale sunsets,—dreary wind,
   Dim shores, dense rains, and heavy-clouded sea !

HINTS ON THE FORMATION OF SMALL LIBRARIES INTENDED FOR PUBLIC USE.

[This paper was prepared by the present writer for the Co-operative Congress, May and June, 1869. It has since been several times reprinted at home and abroad.]

The present age may be characterised as an age of Libraries. Never were they so numerous as at present, and never were they more extensively used. The great libraries of antiquity are more than rivalled by the national collections of England, France, and Russia; in value and in real extent, the British Museum probably exceeds the Alexandrian library; and in addition to these noble institutions, we have now a large and constantly-increasing class of libraries intended for the use of those to whom the doors of the older libraries were rigidly closed. On trying to realise in our mind the immense number of volumes conserved in the national libraries—on thinking of the 602,000 volumes of the British Museum, of the 540,500 vols. of the Imperial library at St. Petersburg,—we can scarcely wonder at the notion which was once current, that in them was stored the sum total of human thought and human learning. The increase of bibliographical knowledge has dissipated this old error, and we now know that no single library can ever hope to make with truth a claim to completeness. The librarians of the largest collections will tell you mournfully of the thousands of volumes which they can never possess, and will confirm the truth of that ancient writer, who declared it would be more easy to empty the ocean, and to count the grains of sand, than to count the number of books existing in the world.

Here, then, we may see the necessity for selection;— a necessity even for the largest of national institutions, but a hundredfold more imperative on smaller libraries.

A mass of books brought together upon no principle, has small claim to be considered a library, and has little chance of producing those humanising and ennobling effects which should flow from such institutions. From want of judgment in the selection of books, too many of our smaller libraries have failed to perform the work their founders intended. By what principles should the promoters be guided? In the formation of a private library, the only guides are the tastes and studies of the possessor; but in one intended for the use of persons of various ages, pursuits, and degrees of culture, there should be an effort at universality; all healthy tastes should be consulted, and (as far as possible) all shades of opinion should be represented; and the student in every department of human knowledge should find there something to aid his researches. Of course this is only possible within certain limits: it needs no art magic to know that a thousand volumes cannot cover the wide field of science and thought; but a thousand volumes, well selected, may certainly furnish an introduction to the sciences, and contain also most of those books which have exercised undying influence on the progress of the human race.

The aim of such a library should be to present an epitome of the entire circle of the sciences, and also to offer to its user those masterpieces of literature which all ages look upon with reverence; and, in addition, as many healthy and interesting and healthy works of fiction and lighter literature as possible. How sadly many small libraries fall short of this ideal how little assistance they can give to those desirous of studying the laws of nature, or of gathering wisdom from the pregnant words of the wise departed,—all who have had any practical acquaintance with them, must be fully aware.

Few of the Co-operative libraries, we should think, will have much less than a thousand volumes on their shelves; and if the aims above indicated are kept steadily in view, it will be possible with that number of volumes to provide information—elementary information at least—on most of the topics which affect the wellbeing or excite the curiosity of mankind. Having thus secured a good foundation, the superstructure may be erected at leisure; but care should be taken not to devote attention to the enrichment of any one class exclusively; a judicious balance should be kept in all parts. But whilst every library should thus aim at an encyclopædic character, each one should have its special characteristics, and it should be a matter of serious consideration as to the precise class to which preference should be given. It is evident that books which in one locality are of great interest and utility, may in another be comparatively worthless. The only rule that can be laid down is—that immediate preference should be given to those works which bear most directly on the interests of those who will have to use them.

It is impossible within the limits of this paper to undertake a survey of the wide field of literature, or to give details as to the precise works desirable in each class. It would be wise, in the first place, to procure a good modern Encyclopædia, such as Chambers's, or the Encyclopædia Britannica, and then such collections as Weale's Rudimentary Series, Knight's Weekly Volumes, Murray's Family Library, &c., &c., and other similar series of concise works on science, history, and general literature. These will fill each class in about equal proportions, and each may be increased as opportunities offer and funds allow.

Co-operative libraries should, it appears to me, give especial attention to social science, and should contain the best information on the various social systems now or formerly in use, and the works of the greatest thinkers who have written on political economy.

After a number of good and serviceable books have been collected, the next care should be their classification for arrangement on the shelves. Now, it may appear a very easy task to arrange a number of volumes, and place together all those which relate to analogous topics; and yet experience shows that it is an extremely difficult operation, and one on which the widest diversity of opinion exists.

Mr. Edwards, who has paid much attention to this subject, and investigated it in a thorough manner, advocates a modification of Bouillaud's scheme, and arranges all the domains of human learning in six divisions:—I. Theology. II. Philosophy (Mental). III. History (Civil and Ecclesiastical), Biography, Voyages, Travels, and Topography. IV. Politics, Law, and Commerce. V. Science and Arts. VI. Literature and Polygraphy (Poetry, Novels, Essays, Encyclopædias, &c.) Variations of this scheme have been used in standard books of bibliography, and in various town libraries. The sub-divisions are too numerous to be here given; but an excellent scheme for the classification of a town library will be found in the second volume of Mr. Edwards' Memoirs of Libraries. One far less elaborate would amply suffice for a small library; and each of the sub-classes should be distinguished by a class letter and and a running number. This plan of having separate sets of numbers for the smaller divisions in preference to the general classes, is one that has not yet been tried; but has the obvious advantage of keeping together on the shelves all those works which relate to the same subject, and prevents them from being lost amidst a host of heterogenous works.

Intimately connected with the welfare of libraries, great or small, is the question of **Catalogues**. The disputes as to the best methods of making catalogues have been so bitter and prolonged, that it is somewhat dangerous ground to enter upon. The chief objection against classed catalogues, is the impossibility of obtaining a permanent scientific classification. All schemes for that purpose are in their very nature artificial, and must sooner or later break down. Another objection is that many books are of such a dubious or complex nature, that it is difficult to decide in what section they are to be looked for. The *Pilgrim's Progress* has not much in common with *Tom Jones*, and yet, if we look to form, they both belong to the class of prose fiction. To the same class, for the same reason, belong such politico-philosophical speculations as *Utopia*, *Oceana*, and *Gaudentio di Lucca*. Many other cases might be cited. Readers may naturally be divided into those who wish to see the works of some particular author, and those who want all the books on some given subject. If the library be a small one, the catalogue of which can be sold at a cheap rate, and with a prospect of soon exhausting the edition, the wants of the public will be best secured by printing in one alphabet the titles of the books, arranged first under the author's names, and second under the names of all the subjects of which they treat; and also, in the case of fiction and literary miscellanies, under the first word of the title—of course excluding articles and prepositions. The last rule should be applied to all works issued without the writer's name; but where the writer of an anonymous book is known, his name should be added in brackets.

In addition to the printed catalogue, one should be kept for consultation at the library, each entry being written on a separate slip, and the additions to the library being catalogued as fast as they are received.

As the proper cataloguing of a library is absolutely
essential to its usefulness, a specimen of the method
here proposed may perhaps be allowable:—

1. G. 10.   Paris: Les Associations Ouvrières en Angle-
   terre (Trades Unions). [Par. L. P. A. d'Orleans
   Comte de Paris.]   Paris.   1869.   12mo.
2. G 10. Associations Ouvrières.   Paris.   1869.
3. G 10. Workmen's Associations.   Paris.   1869.
4. G 10. Trades Unions.   Paris.   1869.
5. G 10. Political Economy.   Trades Unions.   Paris.
   1869.

1. M 9. Jennings:

   An introduction to the knowledge of Medals.   By
the late Rev. David Jennings, D.D.   2nd edition.   Birmingham.   1775.   12mo.

2. M 9. Medals, Knowledge of: Jennings, 1775.
3. M 9. Numismatics, Introduction: by Jennings. 1775.

In some cases it may be requisite to write a dozen
entries for one book, and these entries, written on
separate slips of paper or cardboard, and arranged in
alphabetical order, will combine most of the advantages
of a classified catalogue with the simplicity of an
alphabetical one.   In printing the catalogue, it may
perhaps be required, for the sake of economy, to abridge
the titles under the authors' names; in which case care
must be taken to compress as much information as
possible into the space available.

As our model library has now been carefully selected,
judiciously classified, and well catalogued, we come
next to the system of book-keeping, which should be
as simple as possible.   A register of stock, and a record
of books issued, are indispensable.   The stock books
should be lists of the books in their proper order upon
the shelves, and by these lists the library should be
periodically examined, to see that each article is in its
proper place, and that none are absent without leave.

In the record of issues should be entered the title and number of the book, the name of person to whom, and the date when, it is lent, and the date of its return. This book should be examined daily, to see that no books are detained beyond the time allowed by the rules.

In binding the books, a plain strong binding will be found most serviceable; and in most cases all lettering may be dispensed with. Each book should, if possible, have over its binding a paper cover to protect it, and on this might be written its title and press-mark. Some of these details may appear trivial and unneeded; but it is from lack of system in their formation and management, that many small libraries fail to exercise the beneficial influence which they might otherwise exert. In conclusion: it is important to repeat that the value of a library must depend entirely upon the skill with which it has been selected; and unless efforts are made to give an encyclopædic character to these libraries by a principle of universal selection, some persons, students of some phase of science, will have to be refused that aid which a library should give to all who consult it. And if these libraries are stocked with judgment and discretion, and managed generously and well, it is evident that they may be of great educational use, and have the happiest effects on the intellectual life of those who use them.

THE ART OF CATALOGUING.

It has been said that every man thinks himself competent to drive a gig and to edit a newspaper. To this
may be added "and to catalogue books" It is only by
actual experience that the difficulty of the operation
becomes apparent. One of De Morgan's essays is devoted
to showing the difficulty of describing books correctly.
The initial difficulty of the cataloguer is as to the form
which his work shall assume. There is a prejudice in
favour of a classified arrangement. It has a scientific
appearance, and it is only when the mazy intricacies of
the classes have to be threaded that the fallacy of these
appearances becomes evident Each person has his own
views as to the proper method of dividing human knowledge The Comtist and the Tractarian will not agree
as to the sections into which theological literature shall
be divided. One cataloguer may boldly relegate Chilling-
worth to the corner for heretics and another place side
by side the Gospels and the Book of Mormon. Even
where the *odium theologicum* does not intervene the fluid
condition of human learning must defy all attempts at a
rigid marking out The arts change, new sciences arise,
and old ones fall into disrepute Astrology and Alchemy
which once overshadowed Astronomy and Chemistry are
now discarded by scientific minds Changes in the
political relations of different nations will in the same
way disturb from time to time the most accurate classification of books relating to history and travels. The
arrangement in proximity to each other of works on the
same subject is of course desirable, but it should be at
once confessed that this is only possible as an aid to
memory and not as a genealogical chart of human knowledge Supposing such a logical classification were
devised, the existence of so many books treating of more
than one subject would invalidate its perfection. There

is obviously great difficulty in using classified catalogues from the causes mentioned.

The alphabetical plan is satisfactory only to the bibliographer and not always even to him. It helps to books already known on any given subject but does not enlarge the boundaries of that knowledge. Nor is it unattended with difficulties. It may seem that there can be no hesitation as to the name of an author, and that its allocation in an alphabetical scheme is a matter of almost mechanical ease. Many books however are published without the name of any author at all. Some authors have in the course of their lifetime borne more than one name. Numerous works appear with fictitious names on the title page. These are sometimes mere disguises, at other times frauds. Some books—and famous ones—have been attributed to the pen of half a dozen individuals.

A third school of cataloguers has arisen. Of this Dr. Andrea Crestadoro, the present chief Librarian of the Manchester Free Library, is an able exponent. His views were laid before the public many years ago, and are now being carried into effect in the catalogue of the Free Reference Library.*

A catalogue Dr. Crestadoro regards as having a double function. One is to indicate with all possible exactness the title of every book in the library. The second is to direct the inquirer as speedily as possible to any author and to any subject he may want. The difference in object suggests the advisability of separating the two processes. The first part of the catalogue is called principal entries or inventorial catalogue, the second the index or finding catalogue. The first part need not be in alphabetical order at all. It is immaterial what form

---

* The Art of making Catalogues of Libraries; or a method to obtain in a short time a most perfect, complete, and satisfactory printed catalogue of the British Museum Library, by a Reader therein. London: printed and sold by the Literary, Scientific, and Artistic Reference office, No. 10, Brownlow Street, Holborn, 1856. 8vo. pp. 60.

it takes. It may even be classified. Each entry however must have a consecutive number. The principal entry consists of the title of the book, giving either all the words contained upon the title page, or where space is an object, omitting that surplusage in which some authors —and especially the older ones—delight. All that this entry declares is that a work having such a title is in possession of the library. For the index or "finding catalogue" every subject named upon the title page that is at all likely to be an object of inquiry is made into a brief separate entry. This process results in a concordance of every subject and author named in the titles of all the books in the library. It forms an index of topics which embraces the smallest as well as the largest matters. It does not attempt to fit the books to a Procrustean bed of classification, but adopts the author's own statement as to the subject of his book. It very often happens that a title page does not do this correctly. Some err by excess, and some by under statement, whilst other titles are simply enigmas. These *lacunæ* so far as possible the cataloguer supplies to the principal entry, and his additions become equally material for the index —entries as are the author's own words. The difficulties arising from synonymes, from joint authorship, literary disguises, and changes of name are obviated by cross references in the index. The system resembles the plan that has always been adopted in the calendars of MSS., with the addition of the important element of a concordance-index. The flexibility of the method is greatly in its favour. The principal entries once in type would never need to be reprinted. Each supplementary volume would contain an index of all the principal entries.*

---

* Catalogue of the Books in the Manchester Free Library. Reference Department. Prepared by A. Crestadoro, Ph.D., &c., &c. London, 1864. 8vo. pp. vii., 975. A supplementary volume, as large if not larger, is now in the press and will be especially valuable on account of the number of instances in which the contents of important periodicals, &c., are given.

The plan may be illustrated by titles taken at random from the writer's bookshelves :—

Liste Littéraire Philocophe ou catalogue d'Etude de ce qui a été publié jusqu'a nos jours sur les Sourds-Muets; sur l'oreille, l'ouïe, la voix, le langage, la mimique, les aveugles, etc, etc. Par C. Guyot Dr. en Med. et R T. Guyot Dr. en Droit, Instituteurs de Sourds-Muets, chevaliers de l'ordre du Lion Neerlandais. Groningue : J. Ooomkens, Imprimeur de l'Université. 1842. 8vo. pp. xv., 496, 63. No. 1.

In making the index entries each subject named in the title would be stated as briefly as possible. We should have :—

Deaf-and-Dumb. Catalogue of books relating to. Guyot. Groningue. 1842. No. 1.

There would be similar entries under the name of the authors and under the words "Catalogue," "Ear," "Hearing," "Voice," "Language," "Mimicry," and "Blind." Each of these entries would refer to others of a similar import. Thus the searcher after works treating on Language would be reminded that there were others entered under the words "Speech," "Dialect," and so forth.

The difficulties of classification may be seen in the following longwinded title from which much superfluous matter has been omitted in the parts marked by asterisks.

Polygraphice[1]: or the arts of Drawing[2], Engraving[3], Etching[4], Limning[5], Washing[6] [of Maps and Prints][7], Varnishing[9], Gilding[10], Colouring[11], Dyeing[12], Beautifying[13], and Perfuming[14].** And a Discourse of Perspective[15], Chiromancy[16] and Alchymy[17]. To which is also added, I. The one hundred and twelve Chymical Arcanums[18] of Petrus Johannes Faber[19] ** Translated out of Latin into English. II. An Abstract of Choice Chymical

> Preparations fitted for Vulgar Use for curing most
> [20]
> Diseases incident to Humane Bodies.   The fifth
> edition : enlarged ** Adorned with twenty-four
> copper sculptures; the like never yet extant.   By
> [21]
> William Salmon.**   London, 1685.   8vo.

It will be seen by the figures that twenty index entries
would be required to give clues to all the subjects
treated in this quaint volume, which ranges from the
philosopher's stone to the best method of making "pastils
or crions."   The words in brackets are added to avoid
ambiguity.

If some books err by the garrulity of their title pages,
others are unduly curt.

> Qvintvs Cvrtivs.   Aldvs.   *Colophon.*   Venetii.
> in aedibvs Aldi et Andreae Soceri.   Mense Ivlio
> M.D. XX.   8vo.

Here the cataloguer would need to add the subject of
the book—Alexander—and the name of its editor—F.
Asulanus.

Where the author of an anonymous book is known his
name should be added :—

> Reader! walk up at once (it will soon be too late)
> and buy at a perfectly ruinous rate A Fable for
> Critics ; or, better,—I like as a thing that the reader's
> first fancy may strike, an old-fashioned title page
> such as presents a tabular view of the volume's
> contents :—A Glance at a few of our Literary Pro-
> genies (Mrs. Malaprop's word) from the tub of
> Diogenes ; that is a series of jokes by a Wonderful
> Quiz who accompanies himself with a rub-a-dub-
> dub, full of spirit and grace on the top of the tub.
> Set forth in October, the 21st day, in the year '48, by
> G. P. Putnam, Broadway.   12mo.   pp. iii., 78.

This it will be seen is the now rare original edition of
Lowell's Fable for Critics.   In the same way where
authors have written under assumed names the real
name should be given.   Where a book falsely professes
to be by a certain author the reader should be warned.

The question as to the extent of such additions may safely be left to individual taste. The reader of a catalogue will not be offended at finding there a statement of a fact already familiar to him if he will remember that there was a time when the information would have been a novelty. Catalogues might be made much more useful than they are at present if the "Contents" of books were oftener given, and the subjects indexed. There are many works whose varied interest cannot be surmised from the title page. A single example may suffice:—

> A Memorial of Francis [Foster] Barham. A Selection of Autobiographical and other Compositions from his unpublished MSS., together with a few papers and reports of lectures that have already been published. Edited by Isaac Pitman. London [Bath printed], 1875. 8vo. *Chiefly printed in Phonotypy.*

This work includes, besides poems and autobiographical sketches the following distinct articles and books:— "Plea for Evangelical Education," "On Swedenborg's Theology," "Biblical Conversations or Sacred Remedies for Secular Evils," "Essay on Sacred Poetry," "The Office of the Preacher," "Memoirs of James Pierrepont Greaves," "Essay on Bibliography and Education," "Plea for Union and for Biblical Education," "On the Advancement of Philosophy," "On Divinity; its manifestations and relations," "The Hot Waters of Bath," "Syncretism; its principles and objects," "On the Advancement of Literature, Science, and the Fine Arts," "Essay on Psalmody," "Life and Doctrines of Coleridge," "Alism," "Copernican Astronomy of the Bible," "Translation of Lokman's Arabic Fables," "Life and Times of John Reuchlin," "Rhymed Harmony of the Gospels." The statement of the contents of such miscellaneous books, and of the papers in volumes of "Transactions" and periodicals would add greatly to the usefulness and suggestive of Catalogues. In connection with popular libraries it would probably be an advantage, if to some extent the critical function were exercised, and the inquirer directed to *the* authority on the subject he was "looking up." The young especially waste many valuable hours over second-rate books, simply because there is no one to tell them which is best. The catalogues of the Boston Free Libraries contain from time to time bibliographical notes that form capital guides to the study of the special topics to which they relate.

Bibliography has never received its fair share of recognition in England. Hence the poor and inaccurate book-lists with which many libraries have been content. With a more generous appreciation of the value of bibliography as the handmaid of every science, we shall see these relegated to merited obscurity and in their place we shall have catalogues that will readily give a key that will unlock the hidden wealth of what Ruskin has called King's Treasuries.

DESCRIPTION OF THE PLATES.

The portrait of Humphrey Chetham, of which this is an engraving, is by a contemporary artist, and hangs in the Reading Room of the Chetham Library.

II.

MS. OF MATTHEW PARIS.

The following account of this MS. appeared in the *Manchester Guardian*:—

In the year 1655, some few months after the foundation and establishment of this ancient "free library," a small folio MS. volume (now No. 6,712 of the Catalogue), was presented to it by a "Nicholas Higginbotome, gentleman, and steward of the manor of Stockport." It was entitled, "Flores Historiarum Matthæi Westmonasteriensis, monachi" (The Flowers of History, by Matthew of Westminster, monk). It is beautifully written on vellum, in a hand of the fourteenth century, with illuminations and rubricked initials, covering 301 pages. Upon this MS. Mr. J. O. Halliwell has the following remarks in an appendix to the "Archæologia," vol. xxx. page 527:—"The Chetham Library at Manchester contains many valuable MSS. which appear to be nearly unknown, or at least are not alluded to in the ordinary works on the subjects to which they refer. For instance, a remarkably fine copy of the 'Flores Historiarum' of Matthew of Westminster is preserved there, and possesses a more than ordinary value from its having belonged formerly to the monastery of which its writer was a member, no doubt transcribed in its scriptorium, and contains besides most curious and valuable contemporary historical notes." The best part of the story is yet to be told. Recently that accomplished scholar and antiquary, Sir Frederick Madden, who presides over the Manuscript Department of the British Museum Library, being engaged in a critical investigation into the origin and authorship of the celebrated chronicle which bears the above name, asked to be permitted to have the loan of the Chetham Library MS. for a short time, for the purpose of careful examination. The governors, with a liberality which in one notable local instance has not been shown, granted the loan, and the precious volume was returned a few days ago, with the following "memorandum" in the handwriting of Sir Frederick Madden:—The title prefixed to this volume by its owner in 1657 [? 1655] is erroneous. The work was never known by the name of "Liber Westmonasterii," and the mistake has arisen from finding these words written on the first page of the chronicle in the present MS., which only indicates that the volume then (fourteenth century) belonged to the church of Westminster. This work has hitherto been attributed to a "Matthew of Westminster," who is supposed to have compiled it after the year 1307. This statement rests solely on the authority of Bale, followed by Archbishop Parker, who first printed the work in 1567 (from MS. now in Eton College), and again in 1570, much altered and interpolated. No person, however, of the name of Matthew of Westminster ever existed, and the error was occasioned by finding the name of Matthew (*i.e.*, Paris) as the writer under the year 1250. The adjunct of Westminster is not found in the oldest and best MSS., and indeed is a mere conjecture to be traced to the scribe of a copy made at Norwich in the fourteenth or fifteenth century. From internal evidence, this chronicle was certainly composed at the Abbey of St. Albans down to the year 1265, and the present valuable manuscript affords undeniable evidence of the fact, since it is the original copy of the work, containing an abridgment of the greater chronicles of Wendover and Matthew Paris. It was transcribed under the eye of the latter historian, as proved by the text, from the close of 1241 to near the end of 1249, which is in the handwriting of Matthew Paris himself, as I can with certainty affirm. After the death of Paris, in 1259, the work was continued by another writer at St. Albans to 1265, and subsequently, after the MS. passed into the possession of the church at Westminster, by monks of that Abbey. From evidence I have collected, I am of opinion that this continuation from 1265 to 1306, inclusive, is to be ascribed to John Bevere, otherwise named John of London (who died in 1310), and then from 1307 to 1325 to Robert of Redyng, as appears by the note in the present volume under that year. It must be observed, however, that the text of Bevere as it here appears is abbreviated from his fuller chronicle (in MS. Harl. 641 with which agree MS. Col. Eton, and the first edition of Parker); and that Robert of Redyng appears to have availed himself of the labours of Adam Murimuth after 1313.

(Signed) F. MADDEN.

British Museum, Department of MSS.,
29th March, 1866.

The importance of the facts here affirmed cannot be over-rated. The original MS. of Matthew Paris's "Flowers of History," an old chronicle of great historical value, has rested for more than two centuries in our fine old local library. More than one competent judge of its importance has declared that it ought to be placed in the British Museum ; and we believe we do not at all exaggerate the money value of this volume in placing it at £500. [It would probably fetch double that sum if offered in the market now.]

III.

MS. OF VALERIUS MAXIMUS.

This is a fine folio MS. on vellum, extending to 431 leaves. It is a copy of the French translation of Valerius Maximus made by Symon de Hesdin at the request of Charles V. of France, as is shown by the following :—

> Cy apres commence le liure de valerius maximus translate de latin en francois par Religieuse personne maistre Symon de hesdin maistre en theologie et frere de lospital de saint Jehan de Jherusalem Per Requeste de Charles le quint Roy de france.

It contains the original text also with the prohemium of D. de Burgo. The date is given in the colophon of the first book :—

> Icy fine le translateur du premier liure de valerius maximus auec la declaration deceluy Et additions plusieurs faitte et compilee par frere Symon de hesdin frere de lospital de saint Jehan de Jhrhm dotteur en theologie Lan mil ccclxxv.

The second book is dated 1377, "Le second jour de mai." Alfred Franklin has given a particular account of the copy executed for the King, and which is now in the chief library of France; and there is another copy of this translation, but on paper, in the Benedictine Abbey of Rheinau, in Switzerland. There are some leaves of parchment in it. It forms two folio volumes, and is illustrated with drawings. There is an entry stating that Hesdin translated Valerius to the end of book vii., and that the remainder was by "Nicole de Gonnesse, maistre es ars et en theologie," who apologetically states that his style will be found worse than that of Hesdin   " Et fut finee cette translacion l' an mil iiijc. et ung, laveille de Saint Michel Archangel." Another copy of this translation is in the Jesuit library at Louvain   (See *Biographie Universelle*, tom xlvii. p 316, tom. lxvii p 159)

IV.

CAXTON'S GOLDEN LEGEND.

The fac-simile from Caxton's Golden Legend, first edition, 1483, is from fol. cclxix , where the account of Saint Bartholomew commences.

V.

The autograph of John Byrom, F R S , is from a book in his collection now in the Chetham Library.   The title is ·—

> Jesus is God : or the Deity of Jesus Christ vindi- cated   *   *   By D. Pead.   *   *   Lon- don, 1694.

The book contains a curious reference (p 4) to the cure of Mary Maillard, a " modern miracle " that excited a good deal of attention in its day.

The autograph of Robert Burton is one that rarely occurs.   This has been photographed from a volume in the Free Library, containing —I Montagu's Acts and Monuments, 1642 II. Heylyn's Ecclesia Restaurata, 1661.   Burton has written his name on the title page of each book.

Garrick's bookplate has been copied from " The works of Edmund Waller, 1772," now in the Free Library [24902].

The Shakspere signature is from a volume written by William Henry Ireland, to convince some one who still believed in the authenticity of Vortigern of his ability to fabricate old documents   The volume is in the Free Library [27945]

The signature and motto of Thomas Hearne has been photographed from the flyleaf of the " little London Directory," 1677, now in the Free Library [14305]

The signatures of Delambre and Arago are from a fine copy of Delambre's Histoire de l'Astronomie, Paris, 1817, presented by the author to Olinthus Gregory, and now in the Free Library [30180]

INDEX.

THE END.

LIST OF SUBSCRIBERS.

ALLEY, J. J., Bowdon View, Monton.

ANDREW, FRANK, F.R.H.S., Apsley Place, Ashton-under-Lyne.

ASHTON, THOMAS, Ford Bank, Didsbury.

BAILEY, J. E., F.S.A., Stretford.

BARDSLEY, REV. CHARLES, W., M.A., Hanover-sq., Higher Broughton.

BEARD, JOSEPH, 3, Clifton Terrace, Southend.

BELLOTT, WILLLIAM HENRY, M.D., F.R.C.S.E., Moreton Lodge, Leamington Priors, Warwickshire.

BLEASDALL, REV. JOHN, B.A., Enville Place, Ashton-under-Lyne.

BREMNER, JOHN A., J.P., Hilton House, Prestwich.

BUCKLEY, GEORGE F., Linfitts House, Delph, Near Manchester.

BURTON, J. H., 5, Trafalgar Square, Ashton-under-Lyne.

CHADWICK DAVID, M.P., 64, Cross Street, Manchester.

CHAPMAN, R. A., Regent Road, Salford.

CORNISH, BROS., 37, New-st., Birmingham.

CORNISH, J. E., 33, Piccadilly Manchester.

COWIE, The Very REV. B. M., D.D., Dean of Manchester.

COOPER, JOSEPH, Eaves Knowles, New Mills.

CROMPTON, SAMUEL, M.D., 24, St. Ann's Square, Manchester.

CROSSLEY, JAMES, F.S.A., 2, Cavendish Place.

DAY, T. J., 53, Market Street, Manchester.

DEPEAR, MATTHEW, 66, Oxford-st., Manchester.

DILLON, J., Bollin Tower, Alderley Edge, Cheshire.

DOWNING, WILLIAM, 74, New Street, Birmingham.

EARWAKER, J. P., M.A., F.S.A., Withington, near Manchester.

EASTWOOD, J. A., 114, Everton Road, Chorlton-on-Medlock.

EVANS, JOHN, 17, Brazenose Street, Manchester.

GALLOWAY, JAMES, 7, Mosley Street, Manchester.

GARNETT WILLIAM, Quernmore Park, Lancaster.

GOURLAY, WILLIAM, Bank Villas, Blackburn.

GRATRIX SAMUEL, Alport Town, Manchester.

GREENHALGH, JAMES, Solicitor, Bolton.

GUEST, WILLIAM H., 78, Cross Street, Manchester.

HORNBY, CAPT., F.G.S., Dalton House, Westmorland.

HADFIELD, CHARLES, Examiner Office, Warrington.

HAMILTON, M., 53, York Street, Cheetham, Manchester.

HANSON, GEORGE, Librarian, Rochdale Free Public Library.

HEYWOOD, JOHN, 141, Deansgate, Manchester.

HOLDEN, JAMES P., St. James' Square, Manchester.

JOHNSON, WILLIAM HENRY, 24, Lever-st., Manchester.

KERSHAW, JOHN, Cross Gate, Audenshaw.

KESSELMEYER, C. W., 1, Peter Street, Manchester.

LAYCOCK, WILLIAM, Fieldhead, Higher Crumpsall, Cheetham Hill.

LEYLAND, JOHN, Hindley, near Wigan.

MINSHULL & HUGHES, Eastgate Row, Chester.

MANCHESTER FREE LIBRARY,

MANCHESTER LITERARY CLUB.

MILNER, GEORGE, 59a, Mosley Street.

MAYOR, REV. JOHN E. B., M.A., St. John's College, Cambridge.

MOORHOUSE, CHRISTOPHER, Town Clerk, Salford.

NAPIER, G. W., Merchistoun, Alderley Edge.

NODAL, J. H., The Grange, Heaton Moor.

O'NEILL, ARTHUR, Examiner Office, Manchester.

O'REILLY, JOHN, Livesey Street, Manchester.

PEARSE, PERCIVAL, 8, Sankey Street, Warrington.

POTTER, CHARLES, Werneth, Oldham.

RADFORD, THOMAS, M.D., Moorfield, Higher Broughton.

REID, J., 31, Cornhill, Ipswich.

ROCHDALE FREE PUBLIC LIBRARY.

ROTHWELL, SELIM, India Buildings, 20, Cross Street, Manchester.

RYLANDS, J. PAUL, F.S.A., Highfield, Thelwall, near Warrington.

RYLANDS, W. HENRY, Highfield, Thelwall, near Warrington.

SANDERSON, W. WALBANK, F.R.H.S., Conservative Club, Manchester.

SLAGG, JOHN, 30, Pall Mall, Manchester.

SLATER EDWIN, St. Ann's Square, Manchester.

SMITH, REV. J. FINCH, M.A., Aldridge Rectory, near Walsall.

SMITH & SON, MESSRS. W. H., 73, Market Street, Manchester.

STEINTHAL, REV. S. ALFRED, The Limes, Nelson Street, Chorlton-on-Medlock, Manchester.

SUSSUM, A., Stretford, near Manchester.

SUTTON, C. W., Free Library, Manchester.

TAYLOR, JOHN, Rostherne View, Park Road, Bowdon.

THOMPSON, JOSEPH, 16a, Charlotte Street, Manchester.

TIMMINS, SAM, J.P., F.S A, Elvetham Lodge. Birmingham.

TURNER, J. FOX, Sandiway, Ashton-on-Mersey.

WADSWORTH, GEORGE, 96, Albert-sq., Manchester.

WARBURTON, SAMUEL, Sunny Hill, Crumpsall.

WATTS, JOHN, Ph. D., 23, Strutt Street, Manchester.

WAUGH, EDWIN, 27, Sagar Street, Manchester.

WILKINS, PROFESSOR A. S., M.A., Cassington Road, Victoria Park, Manchester.

WILKINSON, THOMAS READ, F.S.S., The Grange, Didsbury.

WINTERBURN, GEORGE, Deansgate, Bolton.

WOOD, HENRY, 7, St. James' Square, Manchester.

WOOD, RICHARD, John Street Mills, Heywood.

YOUNG, HENRY, 12, South Castle Street, Liverpool.

ERRATA.

Page 2, for " *Monardus* " read " *Monardes.* "

Page 65, line 14, for " *Expliqué* " read " *Expliquée.* "

Page 89—93, for " *Holy Trinity Church* " **read** " *Sacred Trinity Church.* "

Page 91, line 22, for " *o'* " read " *of.* "

Page 104, line 32, delate , after Sharon.

Page 106, line 29, for " *Whittaker* " read " *Whitaker.* "

Page 120, line 23, for " *Barrett* " read " *Barritt.* "

CPSIA information can be obtained at www.ICGtesting.com
Printed in the USA
LVOW03s1844300315

432595LV00014B/376/P